This is Life
"Haik al-Haya"

FIVE YEARS TEACHING IN PALESTINE

CYNTHIA D. YODER

The events and conversations in this book have been set down to the best of the author's ability, although some names and details have been changed to protect the privacy of individuals.

Grateful acknowledgment is made to AAUP for the use of photographs of the university in 2020. All other photographs are courtesy of the author and Robert Gravelin. Except for photos taken in public settings, photographs have been used with consent.

The two maps are based on a United Nations map and a University of Texas Libraries map.

Cover design by EbookPbook

Copyright © 2020 by Cynthia D. Yoder

All rights reserved. No part of this book may be reproduced in any manner without permission in writing from the author, except for the use of brief passages in a book review.

Published by Be Still Press

ISBN: 978-1-7361936-0-0 (Paperback)
ISNB: 978-1-7361936-1-7 (ebook)

For the Palestinian people who befriended me
For Waleed, who inspired me
For Bob, who has been with me all along the way

Palestine

I will always love it
Every time I see it, I feel sad inside
When I see what happened and still happens in it
Palestine is my heart
Is my soul
Is my love

—Student, Arab American University of Palestine

Contents

Preface	ix
Maps	xi

YEAR ONE — **1**

1	First Impressions	3
2	The University Vision	11
3	The Intifada	16
4	Teaching in The Situation	22
5	Learning from Each Other	29
6	A Cold Night Outside	34
7	Wandering the Hills	46
8	Being a Foreigner in Jenin	51

YEAR TWO — **67**

9	A New Year	69
10	No Ink in Palestine	75
11	The Happy Van	81
12	Visits to Jenin Refugee Camp	87
13	Carrying on through Chaos	93
14	Recruiting	101

YEAR THREE — **111**

15	Bob is Back	113
16	English at AAUP	118
17	Loud Voices	122
18	Palestinian Hospitality	125
19	Empowering Students	131
20	Interfaith Relationships	137

YEARS FOUR AND FIVE — **147**

21 Soldiers, Everywhere — 149
22 Political Activism — 156
23 Living in Isolation — 161
24 Intimidation at the Border — 166
25 Death is all Around — 171
26 Turkeys from Talfit — 177
27 Reflection at Graduation — 182
28 A Reminder — 186

Epilogue — 201
Acknowledgments — 203
Notes — 207
A Glossary of Arabic Terms — 209
About the Author — 213

Preface

When I accepted a position at the Arab American University in Jenin, Palestine, I knew that building an English language program from the ground up would be a challenge. What I did not know was that the opening of the university would coincide with a Palestinian political uprising and Israeli response to that uprising which would make our work even more difficult. This book is a memoir of my experience living in Palestine during that challenging time.

After leaving Palestine in January 2006, I wrote the first draft of this story, drawing from my journals and memories. I lived and worked in half a dozen countries after that, and this book saw several drafts over the years. In 2020, while sheltering at home in Mexico due to the Covid-19 pandemic, I was able to bring the book to completion.

During my five years in Palestine, most of my daily interactions were with Palestinians living in the West Bank under military occupation. I also had dear Palestinian friends in Nazareth, who I visited when I could. The perspective I got to know is that of the Palestinians with whom I lived, worked, and socialized. This memoir is a story of what I observed and experienced, how I reacted, what I learned, and how my experiences changed me.

I chose "This is Life," in Arabic "*Haik al-Haya*," as the title of this book because of the prevalence of this expression among Palestinian people. One of my students explained it in writing: *We live in an uneasy area of the world. This is our destiny that we are unable to change, so we must deal with it. Our life shall keep going.* (Note: The vowel sound in "haik" is a long A sound, like in "bake" or "cake.")

The names of students and some university staff members and friends have been changed to protect identities. Student writing, all kept anonymous, is mostly from my own collection, with a few pieces from other teachers and a school publication. Student writing has been kept in its original form except for shortening the text, changes in punctuation and spelling, and occasional changes in word choice to provide consistency and clarity. The Arabic is written according to how my ear hears the colloquial language rather than according to a standard transcription or transliteration system of classical Arabic. A glossary is included. Though the chapters are arranged in groups by year, the story does not follow a tight chronology. Instead, the chapters focus on themes that were significant in my experience. Any misrepresentations, offenses, or mistakes in content or language are my own.

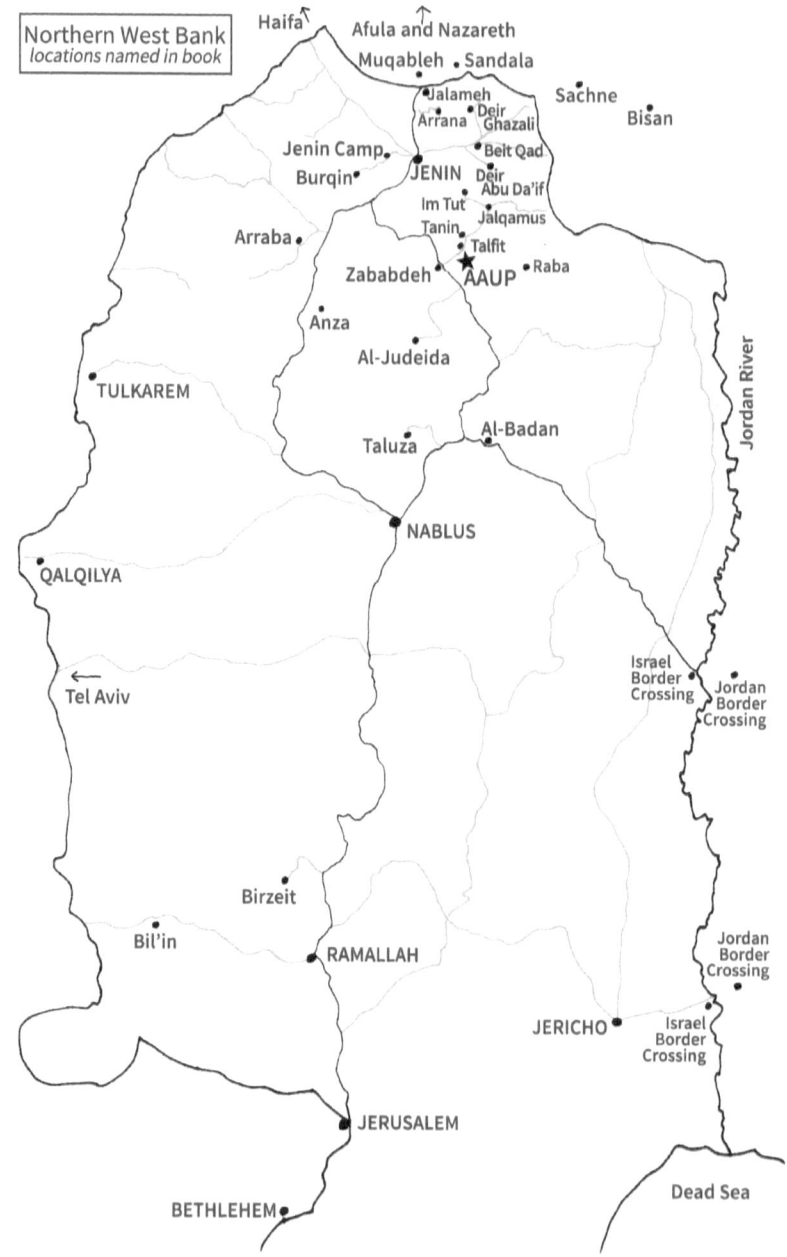

YEAR ONE

Don't Give Up

When you see that the sky is black
And it's very silent around you
Don't give up!
It's only one long night
And tomorrow morning is coming back.

—Student, Arab American University of Palestine

1
First Impressions

He was not much taller than I, and a decade older I guessed, with wavy, trimmed, gray-streaked hair. He stopped to greet me as we bumped into each other in the Vancouver convention hotel lobby. The day before, he had interviewed me for an English-teaching position at AAUJ, the brand new Arab American University of Jenin. Waleed Deeb, the university president, would be my boss if I took the job.

"I'm interested in the position," I told him, "but with one condition."

"What's that?" he asked, his eyes upon mine behind his wire-rimmed glasses.

"I would like to have my own apartment," I replied. At age thirty-nine, I knew what I required.

Looking at me with a smile that would become familiar, Waleed said, "I think that can be arranged."

I had been itching to go overseas again. In the 1980s, I had had my first three-year stint teaching abroad in Egypt. There I had experienced the joy of being myself while living among people of another culture. Since the early 1990s, I had taught English to international students at Eastern Mennonite University in Harrisonburg, Virginia. I had also led EMU study abroad semesters in the Middle East. Those learning experiences with

American college students had taken me to Egypt, Jordan, Israel, and Palestine. I had grown to appreciate the people of the region.

I loved my work at EMU, but I wanted immersion in another culture. Every time a guest speaker from the podium of EMU's chapel shared experiences of living abroad, I asked myself, What am I still doing here? One day, I made up my mind: Now is a good time to go.

After several interviews and job offers, it did not take long to say yes to a post in the West Bank, the land west of the Jordan River bordered by Israel on three sides. In addition to teaching, I would be directing the English Language Center.

Flying into Tel Aviv in July 2000, looking out over the high-rise buildings and dry landscape, I felt excited about this new venture. I was glad that I would be working for someone who seemed flexible, and I was relieved that I would have my own living space. I was anything but relieved, however, when I visited the Palestinian university campus for the first time. It was mid-July, two months before classes would begin. I was enrolled in a short course in Jerusalem and took a day to travel north to the university.

The university sat in the middle of the countryside with hills on all sides, nearly ten miles from the city of Jenin. The faculty apartments stood near a tree-lined road. Construction rubble lay everywhere. An unfinished stairway led up into the four-story building. I remembered my sister-in-law's words as she had hugged me goodbye: "Enjoy the challenge." This apartment building was going to be my first challenge.

I looked away from the apartments to survey the university and the hills in which it was nestled. Four white limestone buildings stood erect and pristine. Beyond the buildings, olive trees with their gnarly trunks stretched out in one direction, and dusty almond trees sprawled out in another. Rocks and occasional bushes covered the sun-baked land. A shepherd's tent in the distance blended into the terrain. A small village sat atop a hill. There's something beautiful about the simple landscape, I thought, anticipating my new life. I tried not to think about the unfinished apartments.

It would be a few weeks before I would begin work and several more weeks before the other new teachers and I would move into our apartments. Jenin had no hotels, so once work began in mid-August, the university put us up in a hotel in the city of Nablus, thirty miles to the south. A driver chauffeured us back and forth to work every day in his van, forty-five minutes each way.

Heading north towards Jenin in the mornings, we twisted and turned as curving roads stretched through hills and valleys with ancient rock formations. An old stone fort and a decrepit Ferris wheel sat out in the middle of nowhere. The stench of burning garbage rose from a huge dump beside the road. Villages teemed with brightly dressed children on their way to school and vegetable vendors setting up their rickety carts. Car horns honked, and voices from mosques sounded the Islamic call to prayer.

We thought we would die from the ninety-degree heat in the van. Each day became a bad hair day for me with the wind whipping in through the windows. Outside the windows, however, lay the rich life of Palestine.

The best thing about those van rides, especially in the afternoons, was the chance to debrief with the others, two college English teachers and four schoolteachers, all new to Palestine. The Arab American University project included an Arab American School housed on the same campus. University classes had not yet begun, but the school was in session. We laughed a lot as the schoolteachers shared crazy stories from their beginning days with the children.

In that van, I first felt a spark of attraction to Robert Gravelin, who would later become my husband. Bob taught art and music in Grades K-8 at the new school. With his wavy and luxurious brown hair, round wire rims framing his tawny eyes, gray Vans sneakers on his feet, and a comfortable way with himself, he often exited the vehicle early on our way home from work to stop for a swim at Al-Badan, a cool valley spring between Jenin and Nablus. I thought, I like his independent spirit and the fact that he likes to swim.

At work at the university, I entered the red-roofed administrative building through its three stone arches. Venturing out from my office each day, I smelled the fresh paint as I walked through the beige halls. I talked with faculty in various departments. Each office was new, so not much hung on the walls. I met Palestinian staff in the President's Suite, Personnel Affairs, Financial Affairs, Purchasing, Public Relations, Registration, Academic Affairs, and the library.

Ibrahim, a stocky young staff member in the library, seized the chance to practice English with a native speaker. Like others, he stopped by my office for short chats or language lessons. "Hello, Miss Cynthia," he said. "If you have time, can I practice my English with you?" I felt happy to get to know my new Palestinian colleagues. Bonds seemed to form quickly.

Several Palestinian women on staff invited me over within weeks; so easy-going were they with their welcomes. "I'd like to invite you to my house," said Nabeela, a staff member in her twenties from the registrar's office. Her straight black hair hung just above her shoulders. Glasses and a big smile decorated her face. One day after work, we traveled by *servees*, the common shared taxi, to her home village, Arraba, thirty minutes away. She introduced me to her husband and young sons. In her simple yet tidy home, we ate chicken with potatoes, sipped tea, and shared life stories. How nice to have a new friend, I thought, when I returned home that night.

"When can you come to my house in Jenin?" asked Leen, the president's secretary. Leen was petite in stature and years, fresh out of college and recently married. She wore Islamic attire. The *hijab,* or head scarf, covered her hair and was pulled tight around her thin face. The *jilbab,* the long, loose outer garment with its flowing folds, covered her clothing underneath. She chose sage green, light blue, and gray. When she invited me home, she opened the door to strong friendship. She took her outer garment off and let her guard down, and I saw a woman just like me.

The half dozen other new teachers and I finally moved into our apartments. The shiny off-white curtains blended into the creamy walls. The stiffness of the tan and rust plaid sofa forced me to sit up straight. My first dinner guests sat on varnished end tables from the living room, since our metal kitchen chairs with vinyl cushions had not yet arrived. Hot water did not appear for over a week.

The mattress label claimed it was *the best in the world*. "That means it's the worst," Waleed said dryly one evening as a group of us sat bemoaning our apartments. Waleed and several other Palestinians from abroad lived in the same building with the same apartment furnishings.

Knowing that I needed a good bed and a place that felt cozy, I bought a firm new mattress and a comfy, cobalt blue sofa set. Bright carpets, yellow pillows, and wall décor changed the apartment into a warm space, a place that I would call home for five years.

The hardest part during those first weeks of living on the hill, as it came to be known, was the constant hum of the generator stationed outside my bedroom window. The generator was important, with no electric lines at the university at that time, but I never got used to its drone. It kept me awake for hours.

When I expressed concern to a manager, Lufti, he retorted, "Don't tell me you can't sleep! And don't compare this to America!" Not having mentioned America, I knew I would not find an ally in Lufti.

Reporting this incident to Waleed, he replied, "You do nag a lot." I felt my eyes well up. What he called nagging, I called persistence. That persistence would get a lot accomplished over the next five years.

When I was escorted to my office on my first day at work, I found a desk, a chair, and a bookshelf. No computer, telephone, fan, or bulletin board. But the building was new and clean, and my office was spacious.

That day I bonded with the laborers, Rihab and Jamal, as we went up and down the stairs several times together with the ten boxes of teaching materials that I had shipped ahead. Raised with a Mennonite work ethic, I was not in the habit of standing around watching other people work. Many eyes were upon me that morning—a woman, a foreigner, a director carrying boxes. Especially the beady eyes of Rauf, the short, balding supervisor who seemed to love telling the laborers what to do. Even if Rauf thought he was someone special, I would later realize the importance of staying on his good side, since I would often need his help.

I had much to do! I made lists and checked things off, glad for the time before classes started to get organized. Simple tasks were a challenge. We lacked what I considered necessities, like computer equipment or a stable electric current. Without an office computer, I carried my Sony VAIO laptop and Hewlett Packard printer like an infant in my arms back and forth to work each day. Three minutes was all it took between home and work. As I walked along the narrow path, gardeners plucked away at the dirt, arranged rocks in small circles, and watered young trees in the centers. *"Marhaba,"* I greeted them with an Arabic hello.

My step counter was a favorite possession that semester. A record-keeper like my father, I kept track of my steps with my pedometer, reaching 17,000 one day. Sulaiman, the head of maintenance, was intrigued with the gizmo, a rather new gadget at that time. In another year, I would bring Sulaiman his own pedometer. Sulaiman's dark eyebrows and dark mustache stood out on his face, while his plaid shirts identified him. I was sure his daily steps outnumbered mine.

Early one morning in the copy center, I discovered that there was no paper. This was not the first time. To get paper, I needed to get approval from the president himself, by obtaining his signature. I heard the annoying words, "You must get Dr. Waleed's signature" so many times that the next autumn, I would come back with T-shirts made for Waleed and several colleagues displaying the words *Get Waleed's signature* beside a red stop sign. Having the chance to talk to Waleed about *important* matters proved hard enough, let alone asking him for copy machine paper.

The back of the T-shirts revealed *Ask Jim.* When Waleed tired of my questions, he referred me to James Thomas, his senior advisor, whose office was across the hall. Jim, a professor of agriculture and international development from Utah State University, had years of international experience. He aided Waleed and the university in countless ways for two years. His title suited him perfectly—students and faculty alike turned to this hefty man with a perpetual smile for his listening ear and sage advice. *Ask Jim* became a joke between Waleed and me.

One hot afternoon a week or two into my job, I finally had an appointment scheduled with Waleed. I sat down in one of the four black leather chairs in Waleed's office, and he rang for tea. He wore khaki pants, a polo shirt, and suede shoes. In the winter, he would wear sweaters. On his corner hall tree, a tie and sport jacket hung, ready when formality called.

Suddenly, five burly men wearing polyester pants and shiny shoes paraded in. They interrupted our conversation with their thunderous hellos, made small talk with Waleed, and ignored me. Is it because I'm a woman or because I'm a white woman with short blond hair that these men are disregarding me? I wondered. This is going to take some getting used to, I thought.

While I did not know how I felt about the overpowering men, Waleed already had my respect. I admired him for what he had helped accomplish thus far in this huge educational endeavor. He had left the U.S. in his fifties to work in Palestine. I just hoped that next time, he would set the men straight.

"Keep all chins up," Jim suggested when I told him of the episode. I did not realize at the time how often I would need to heed Jim's words of wisdom, as well as my sister-in-law's parting words to me.

2

The University Vision

Amidst papers on President Waleed Deeb's desk and coffee table, lay wooden puzzles and other brain teasers. When I visited Palestinian families with Waleed, I noticed how he paid attention to the children. In addition to playing games with them, he gave them math problems and other puzzles to figure out.

He reminds me of Grandpa Hartzler, I thought, also a professor of mathematics. In his letters to me as a child, my grandpa had always sent story problems.

Critical thinking was so important to Waleed that he organized what he called thinkshops for students and teachers throughout Palestine. He also established *Al-Muntada*—The Young Scientists Club—to develop thinking skills in children and teens.

Waleed was a private man who did not often boast his accomplishments. In time, however, I learned from this soft-spoken man about both his passions and the history of the university.

In 1996, Waleed was approached about being involved in the venture of a new university, the first private university in Palestine. He eventually agreed, on the condition that the university be a place of free thought. He had just spent a year as a visiting professor at Birzeit University in Ramallah, a major West Bank city. During that year, he also helped revamp the mathematics portion of the Palestinian national curriculum for Grades 1-12.

In Waleed's mind, a critical thinking and creativity component was crucial to that curriculum. He believed that rather than memorizing facts and giving the "right" answer, which was the norm in the old system, students needed to learn to solve problems and seek knowledge on their own.

Waleed joined the university project four years before it opened, hopeful that this university could make a difference in the lives of many young Palestinians. He envisioned an institution that would promote not only critical thinking but also freedom of expression. Science, technology, and research would be emphasized with a modern library and labs where students would learn by doing. Faculty who were also researchers and thinkers would be hired. Since English had become the dominant language of science and technology, English would be the medium of instruction, and students would achieve a high level of English language proficiency. All this would help them to secure good jobs in the future and to make significant contributions in their fields.

In addition, Waleed hoped that at this university, students would focus on being students, rather than representatives of Palestinian political groups, like Fatah and Hamas. Violence would not be an option, and students would respect university property, institutional regulations, and all people.

The university fostered an agreement with California State University at Stanislaus and an affiliation with Utah State University. One intention of such relationships was to have an exchange of students and faculty. Jim Thomas, as well as a handful of USU professors in various fields, came to the Palestinian university to work.

Waleed was an American Jordanian of Palestinian origin. He had spent most of his life in Jordan, Kuwait, Saudi Arabia, and the United States, where he received his education and was a professor of mathematics for many years. This undertaking in Palestine brought him back to his roots.

The original university name, the Arab American University of Jenin, AAUJ, would later be changed to the Arab American University of Palestine, AAUP. In Arabic, it was referred to as simply the Arab American University.

The Jenin governorate, one of eleven districts in the West Bank, was chosen as the location of the university. Jenin was selected in part because there were no other universities in the area and in part because Jenin was close to major Arab cities in Israel, which meant Israeli Arabs might join the university. In addition, the visionary who came up with the idea of the university, Maher Irshaid, owned land in the area. The campus was not actually in the city of Jenin, but eight miles south of Jenin and one mile east of the town of Zababdeh.

A university in the Jenin district would make it easier for high school graduates from the area to attend college. Before AAUP opened, students from Jenin typically attended An-Najah University in Nablus, about thirty miles away, or Birzeit University in Ramallah, about seventy-five miles away. Because of frequent checkpoints and road closures due to the political situation, commuting to school was not always easy. For female students, it was sometimes even more difficult, Jenin being more traditional and conservative than some Palestinian cities. A new university would give added opportunities to young people to pursue a degree.

The university would also impact the city of Jenin and the surrounding communities economically, socially, and culturally.

In addition to the university, the elementary school developed at the same time and built in the same location was unique in that it would be co-educational and would hire some of its teachers from abroad. The school was where Bob and the other new teachers who shared the van rides in the early weeks worked.

I knew from previous experience that Palestinians placed a high value on education. In my Intermediate English class, I asked students to explain why education was important to them. Though the young men and women were just learning how to express their ideas in written English, I could understand their thoughts about education:

The education is important because it give me culture in my life. The education give me more information. The education give me any language. When I transport to any country, I speak to anyone in the country in any language he speaks it. When I have education, I have anything I like to do it. The education give me good job in the life and enjoy when I go to my work.

The education important to me because I can develop myself. I need to learn to be a doctor in the future and get a job. The second thing is when I learn, I can talk to anyone in this world. So education is useful and important. If I learn, I can get happy in my life. The happy is not limited to me.

Everybody in the university put in his mind to study to be a good person in this life. And to get the money that is important to build his life. Finally, he enter the university to build his country and make his society the best persons in the world.

Next, I wanted to find out why my students had chosen to attend AAUP. One day during a class discussion with Advanced English students, I asked, "Why did you decide to study here, at the Arab American University?"

"I want to learn dentistry," said one.

"Because many of the doctors (my students' term for professors) studied in America and Europe, and they are experts," replied another.

"The equipment here is excellent," chimed in a third.

"I want to have strong English language so in the future I can find a good job."

"Because if I graduate from this university, I can study in graduate school in America after that."

"If I graduate from an American university, I will have a better chance of getting a good job, maybe with a foreign company."

My students seemed happy to be at this university. I hoped we could meet their expectations.

3

The Intifada

Why is he pointing his gun at Bob like that? I gasped inside my head, holding my breath. Everyone on the small bus remained still.

About ten of us international teachers were on a weekly shopping trip to Jenin when two young Israeli soldiers stopped our minibus just outside our nearby town, Zababdeh, and stepped inside. The first said a few words in Arabic to our driver. The second said nothing but eyed us teachers. He looked first on one side of the bus and then across the aisle. All the while, his rifle was hanging at his side, aimed directly at Bob's chest.

After a minute or two of checking us out, showing us who was in control, the two soldiers exited the bus, and we looked at one other, breathing sighs of relief.

"Did the guy even know where his gun was aimed?" Bob blurted out to no one in particular. "He had no clue. He was oblivious. Did you notice how young they were?"

We did not know it at the time, but facing soldiers, young and old, wielding guns was going to be our life.

As a pacifist, I disapproved of even toy guns, yet I would be forced to get used to not only seeing guns everywhere but also having guns pointed at me. I came to know that at all stationary checkpoints, it was the job of one soldier to keep a rifle at the ready, levelled directly at whoever was approaching the checkpoint.

Checkpoints obstructed life for me, my students, my colleagues, and everyone living in the region. Stationary checkpoints had set locations. They dotted the West Bank, an area the size of the state of Delaware and home to about two million people at the time. "Pop-up" checkpoints were different in that they could appear on any road at any time.

The Palestinian-Israeli conflict is longstanding and complex. Both sides have historical traumas that have shaped their worldviews.

The Jewish people were mistreated over millennia. As a religious minority living in Europe, Jews were forced to convert to Christianity, restricted from many professions, prohibited from owning land, persecuted, and exiled. They were killed in pogroms, the Inquisition, and the Holocaust. In 1896, the idea of Zionism, a Jewish State, was first put forth. In 1917, the British government offered support for the establishment of a home for the Jewish people in Palestine.

After World War I, the League of Nations gave the British rule over Palestine. The British Mandate, as it was called, lasted from 1923 to 1948. After the British sought to end their mandate, the United Nations got involved. The United Nations created a partition plan in 1947 which would divide the region into Jewish and Arab States. The U.N. Partition Plan would give 55% of the land to the Jews, who comprised about one-third of the population. The Arabs, who made up about two-thirds of the population, would be given 45% of the land.

Historically, Jews and Arabs had lived peacefully on the land. But violence between the majority Arabs and the minority Jews broke out at various points in the 1930s and 1940s. On May 14,

1948, the Jews declared their independence as a state, and the next day, the British left. War ensued between Israel and nearby Arab countries: Egypt, Iraq, Jordan, Lebanon, and Syria. Jewish Israelis refer to the war as the War of Independence, while Palestinians refer to it as the Catastrophe, *Al-Nakba* in Arabic.

According to the Anti-Defamation League, during the war, 750,000 Palestinians fled or were forced to flee from their homes and land, and during the war and after, 800,000 Jews fled or were forced to flee from the Arab countries where they lived due to anti-Zionist violence.[1]

According to the Palestinian Central Bureau of Statistics, it was 800,000 Palestinians who were displaced from a population of 1.4 million. The Israeli army killed 15,000 Palestinians and destroyed 530 Palestinian towns and villages.[2]

When the state of Israel was created, Israel had 77% of the land of historical Palestine, as reported by the United Nations.[3] Jordan controlled the land west of the Jordan River and called it the West Bank, while Egypt controlled the Gaza Strip, or Gaza.

In 1967, after Israel won the Six-Day War, Israel took control of even more land. Israel annexed East Jerusalem, and the Israeli army occupied the West Bank and Gaza, areas that had been granted to the Palestinians in the 1947 U.N. Partition Plan. The United Nations calls this land the Occupied Palestinian Territory.

The Israeli military occupation changed life drastically for those living in the West Bank and Gaza. Palestinians began to have minimal control over their lives. Checkpoints controlled by Israeli soldiers were set up throughout the region, frequently preventing Palestinians from getting to their jobs, their schools, or hospitals. In addition, Palestinian land was confiscated, and homes were demolished.

In 1987, twenty years after the occupation started, a Palestinian uprising called the *intifada* was born. The Arabic word *intifada* in this context means "shaking off." Palestinians sought to shake off the occupying forces and achieve independence from Israel.

In 1993, Israeli Prime Minister, Yitzhak Rabin, and Palestinian Liberation Organization leader, Yasser Arafat, signed an agreement begun in Oslo, Norway called the Oslo I Accords. Each side agreed to recognize the other as a negotiating partner, the starting place for a potential diplomatic peace process.

The two sides deferred negotiations on what are called final status issues, including the borders of Israel and Palestine, the status of Jerusalem, Israeli settlements, water rights, and the right of return of Palestinians to their land.

The 1995 Oslo II Accords divided the West Bank into three areas: A, B, and C. Palestinians were to have complete civil and security control in Area A, which makes up about 18% of the West Bank. Jenin and the Arab American University are in Area A. Israelis were to control Area C, which comprises roughly 60% of the West Bank and is the area where scores of Jewish settlements have been established. In Area B, which makes up around 22% of the West Bank, Palestinians were to have civil control, and Israel was to have control of security.

The Oslo divisions did not give Palestinians in the West Bank freedom of movement. On the contrary, the divisions allowed Israel to restrict Palestinian movement within the occupied territory even more, isolating Palestinians from each other and the outside world. In addition, Israel owns most of the water rights in the West Bank, and Palestinians cannot not dig new wells without permission. The situation in the occupied territory after Oslo has been compared to apartheid, where Palestinians live under control and domination. The two sides in the conflict are far from equal.

A colleague explained the Palestinian point of view to me: "We should not have to pay the price for the Jews' historical suffering. We did not cause their misery."

On September 28, 2000, after the new teachers and I had been there about six weeks, the Arab American University held an opening ceremony on the newly built campus. Excitement filled the air that night as speakers touted the good this institution would bring. Students, their families, faculty, staff, and members of the community listened expectantly that warm autumn evening.

Ironically, earlier that same day, Ariel Sharon, the Israeli opposition leader at the time who would later become Prime Minister, made a move that would further break down the chances for a peaceful resolution to the Israeli-Palestinian conflict. Accompanied by hundreds of armed police officers, Sharon visited a contested area in Jerusalem known as the Temple Mount by Jews and the Noble Sanctuary by Muslims, or *Al-Haram Al-Sharif* in Arabic. The complex, which houses *Al-Aqsa* Mosque and the Dome of the Rock, is a sacred site in Islam.

Sharon's visit to the Islamic holy site was considered a provocation by Palestinians, and the second intifada, or Palestinian resistance movement, began. Though the movement started with stone throwing, it quickly turned violent. What ensued was almost five years of retaliation upon retaliation by Israeli military forces and Palestinians. According to the Israeli human rights group, B'Tselem, over 3,000 Palestinians and nearly 1,000 Israelis would be killed during the uprising, from the end of September 2000 until the beginning of 2005.[4]

Life in the region was already difficult, but the intifada and the Israeli responses to the intifada made it more difficult. Palestinians going about their daily business were frequently held up at checkpoints, and roads were closed. Getting from Point A to Point B was challenging, if even possible. Israeli citizens felt insecure as attacks against them increased. Thus began a new chapter in the lives of many—Palestinians, Israelis, and teachers like me—and a new chapter in the life of the Arab American University.

4

Teaching in The Situation

In Palestine, my students were absent much of the time, and their reasons never ceased to amaze me. One morning Mustafa, a lanky young man from a town west of Jenin, came to Intermediate English after several days of absence. Mustafa usually wore a grin on his face and was a pleasant student, though he liked to sit in the back row and joke around with his buddies. I had not heard that anything out of the ordinary had happened to him, and I wanted to follow the university's mandate to maintain high standards for our students.

"Where have you been, Mustafa?" I asked, assuming he had been skipping class.

"I was with my friend in the hospital. The Israeli soldiers shoot him in the face," he uttered with visible gloom. "He lose half of his face, and four days after, he die."

How can I respond to that? I wondered. I stumbled to express how sorry I was and went home that evening to ponder my own impatience with students when they missed class. It took several weeks for the realities that my students faced to sink in and for me to understand that my sensitivity was of utmost importance.

This was all new to me. In my previous teaching experiences, students generally came to class. If someone was absent, it was usually due to illness or a problem with a girlfriend or boyfriend.

The reasons my students in Palestine missed class were like none I had ever known.

Mahir, a fervent student in my 9:00 a.m. Beginning English class, appeared in my office one day after 10:00. I was sitting behind my desk. "Hi, Mahir. I missed you in class today," I said.

"Hi, Miss Cynthia. I am very sorry I could not reach to class on time. I leave my house at 6:00 to reach the university at 8:00. But an Israeli soldier stop me and keep me waiting for two hours while he check my ID. I reach to the university at 10:00."

"I'm sorry about that, Mahir. I'll show you what we did in class today," I answered. I wondered how a soldier could hold up such a nice guy. Mahir was tall with broad shoulders and well groomed with crisp, ironed shirts always tucked in neatly. His eyes were alive. When I came to class each day, I found him sitting in front with his textbook open.

Mahir was from one of the Palestinian communities in Israel that had struggled to stay when Israel had established itself as a state and taken over many Palestinian towns and villages. People in this minority group self-identify as Palestinians, Israeli Arabs, Arab Israelis, or Israelis. On campus, they could be criticized for not understanding the plight of Palestinians in the West Bank. At the same time, they were often discriminated against in Israel and had their own experience of suffering.

The weekend at AAUP was Thursday and Friday. Friday was the day of prayer for Muslims and the official day off in the country. Saturday was the first day of the week at school and work. One Saturday afternoon, I ran into Naeem, a fit-looking student from Jerusalem dressed in his jeans, T-shirt, and soft-soled shoes that set him apart from Jenin students, who wore polyester pants, nylon shirts, and dress shoes. Naeem was always smiling and wowing me with his knack for American English idioms, like "What's up?" or "How's it going?"

"Where were you this morning?" I asked, remembering his absence from class.

"I went home to Jerusalem this weekend to visit my family, and it took five hours to get here today. Can you imagine, Miss Cynthia, five hours on the road, when it usually takes one hour and a half?"

"That's terrible, Naeem. I'm very sorry," I offered, then asked him about the checkpoints and about his family. Students and colleagues often said, "How is your family? Please say hello to them," even though they had never met them. I tried to do the same.

Since I lived in an apartment on campus and did not travel much, I had not encountered Israeli checkpoints, restricted movement, and humiliation from Israeli soldiers to the extent that my students had. I would have my own travel and checkpoint stories to tell later, but at that time, I was just trying to take it all in. I listened to my students' stories with concern and admiration. Their determination to show up for class in the face of incredible obstacles was remarkable. I could hardly imagine having that kind of perseverance.

At the same time, part of my role was to distinguish between the students with legitimate excuses and the slackers, those who took advantage of the political situation to skip class. Sometimes, students admitted to oversleeping or leaving home late. Others just said, "You know our situation, Miss," or "There was a checkpoint, Miss." It was hard to know if the reasons were valid.

The Student Affairs Office created an excuse form to assist instructors. Students were asked to check one of four boxes indicating the reason for their absence from class: (1) curfew, (2) checkpoint, (3) arrest, or (4) other. The form reminded me of the reality that we were living in.

Wanting to maintain high standards in my classroom, I sometimes sent students to the Student Affairs Office when they missed class. But I usually trusted my intuition and made the judgment myself, knowing that it was better to give my students the benefit of the doubt.

The intifada began on the last Saturday of September 2000. When English classes began a few days later, the regional violence had escalated, and forty Palestinians had been killed. I kept track of the number dead in my date book in the early days: forty dead by Monday, sixty-three by Thursday, eighty by Saturday, and so on until 120 had died in three weeks.

I realized after one or two days in the classroom that I would need to forego my normal lesson plans, which integrated reading, writing, listening, and speaking and also addressed grammar, vocabulary, and pronunciation. I realized that writing topic sentences, practicing skimming and scanning skills, reviewing past tense irregular verbs, and identifying prefixes and suffixes would be meaningless without first acknowledging the deaths and what was happening all over the region, that is, "on the ground."

"Tell me what happened over the weekend," I said to my class after they had settled into their seats one Saturday. Both male and female students told me about the Israeli tank that opened fire in their village and killed a young boy and about the funeral that followed the next day. They described how they tried to travel but were held up at an Israeli checkpoint and how the soldiers slapped and threatened them. They detailed the jeep that spread tear gas and the children that threw stones. They lamented that their neighbor's house was damaged, and their neighbor was arrested.

As students gave me this information, I wrote the key words on the board—Israeli, soldier, shoot, shot, was injured, was killed, die, died. My blackboard became a collage of military terms—tank, jeep, gun, rifle, pushed, interrogated, detained, arrested. The next day, I began class again with "Tell me what happened last night," adding, "Try to use the past tense of the verbs when you are talking about yesterday."

A week following the start of the intifada, I walked home in the late afternoon, weary about everything. I had asked my students that morning to arrange their chairs in a circle and had then sat down with them and said, "Tell me what you think about what is going on."

"You see what the Jewish do to us?" they blasted. "You see how they treat us? The Jewish want to take all our land. They want to kill us. They kill our children. Do we deserve this?"

Suddenly, one of my students reversed the roles and asked me, "What do *you* think?" The others quickly nodded their heads, chiming in, "Yes, what do *you* think?"

"I think what is going on is terrible!" I answered. I think all killing is wrong. I think it is wrong for the Israeli army to kill Palestinians, and I think it is wrong for Palestinians to kill Israelis."

I did not know that my last line would create such a storm. The students began attacking me: "How can you say that after what they do to us? Why do you blame us? Why does your government support Israel? Now you understand why we hate America!"

I had not been prepared for an outrage directed at me. I thought my students might appreciate the fact that I was there with them in Palestine. But I was naive. I quickly learned that other than to express support for and solidarity with my students, saying less was better than saying more. My students did not need pat answers from me. They needed to express their feelings, and it was my job to give them the chance.

Even though I had a negative gut-level reaction to my students' use of the pronoun "they," believing that stereotypes should be avoided, I realized that the classroom was not going to be the place for me to talk about the good Jews I knew. The classroom was not the place for me to suggest that in the media, it was possible to find perspectives from both sides of the conflict. Every time I tried to offer a comment or opinion in those days, the more I learned to be quiet and listen. Then I came to the profound realization: I am here to listen.

Outside the classroom, it was the same. "What did we get from violence?" I asked a Palestinian colleague one day in the hall. I was distraught about the violence that Palestinians were directing against Israelis in their suicide bombings.

"What did we get from peace?" came her enlightening reply. Once again, I discovered that being a listener might be my most important role.

The other teachers and I began creating classroom materials related to *Al-Wade'*, meaning "The Situation." I heard those words in both Arabic and English perhaps more than any other words during my years at the university. "What is the situation *today*? How is the situation on the ground *now*? Let's talk about the *situation*. Tell me about the *situation*. This is what we need to do *right now* in the situation. How can we *deal* with the situation? How do *you* deal with the situation? How are you *doing* in the situation? We have to think of creative *solutions* in our situation. This is *because of* the situation. Teacher, you *know* our situation! You see our *situation*?" No matter where the stress was placed or rising intonation lay, The Situation infused all of life for me, my students, my colleagues, and my friends.

The other words I heard as often were "This is life," in Arabic "*Haik al-haya.*" My students and Palestinian colleagues recited this mantra each day, whenever they spoke of *Al-Wade'*. As one of the English teachers put it, "*Haik al-haya* is our daily bread."

"This is life. What can we do?" Palestinian resilience shone through their humiliation. "This is life" became my mantra too, and the mantra for anyone living there.

5

Learning from Each Other

Boys on one side. Girls on the other. That is how I found my students seated in class as the semester began. Referring to male and female college students as boys and girls was the cultural norm.

Most students were not accustomed to being with classmates of the opposite gender, having attended public schools segregated into male and female. It would take time for them to get used to a co-educational environment. Since the university was new, we had only first-year students, most of whom were just out of high school, eighteen or nineteen years old. About one-third were female.

Working in groups was a novelty as well. When I asked a class to divide into groups, mixing females and males, some of the students looked uncomfortable. "Our holy book, the Quran, does not permit girls to work with boys," a female student said, her friends nodding in accord.

"We agree, Teacher," piped up a male student, grinning at his cohorts. "That is against our religion."

While Christians made up a small percentage of the student population, around five percent, the majority at AAUP were Muslims.

Seeing the deeply ingrained religious and cultural tradition of gender separation, I needed to slow down and re-examine my expectations. I tried not to push but did encourage my students to work together in mixed-gender groups. Some in the class were agreeable from the start, while the hesitation of others diminished in time. Work in mixed-gender groups became routine.

From the first day of class, one female student parked herself on the male side of the room, chewing her gum, rocking her crossed jean-covered leg up and down, showing off her fancy shoes. She reminded me that not everyone thinks alike, an important truth to remember living in another culture, where it can be easy to generalize.

Clothing styles on campus were another reminder of individuality and the broad spectrum of religious belief and practice. Some females sported short skirts and sleeveless tops, while others donned the *jilbab,* or long Islamic outer garment. Some Muslims wore the *hijab,* or head covering, while others did not.

Seeing a Palestinian friend with her head covered one day, I was surprised, unaware that she had been thinking about wearing the *hijab.* "I feel good because I know I did the right thing," she stated. "But my husband is not happy about it."

In my years in Palestine, several friends decided to wear the *hijab* and explained how they made the choice. Other friends kept their hair uncovered.

There was no standard style of dress for a *muhajaba,* a woman wearing the *hijab.* Even a *muhajaba* could wear tight jeans, a tight-fitting blouse, high heels, and makeup. At the university, the students wearing miniskirts caused the biggest scandal.

A group of students pressured Waleed to implement a dress code. When I asked one class what they thought of that idea, a female student wrote, *I think AAUP should have a dress code so it could look like a university, not like a party.* I did not know at that time that the issue would escalate in another year, with leaflets calling for girls to dress modestly. But I knew that Waleed had no intentions of implementing a dress code, going against the very principle of free thought and expression upon which the university had been founded.

Neither was there a written dress code for international teachers. We tried to blend in but still stood out with our light hair and a more casual style of dress. We women dressed modestly in pants or skirts with tops that we hoped would offend no one. Even when the weather was hot, and our offices and classrooms were sweltering, female teachers stayed away from sleeveless tops or short skirts, and male teachers did not wear shorts. In the winter months, dressing modestly was not a problem. I usually bundled up in layers with a scarf around my neck to try to stay warm at work.

Students expressed their religious natures in ways other than clothing styles. Some wrote *Bismallah al-rahman al-raheem*, meaning "In the name of God, the most merciful, the most gracious," in flowing Arabic script at the top of written assignments or splayed across the width of the entire chalkboard. To render their calligraphy more stunning, they used the side of the chalk, making the thin stick of remaining chalk nearly unusable for the instructor. The script on the blackboard was a reminder of the strong faith culture of my students. But I was not always sensitive enough to that culture.

For our Movie Hour, we chose films we thought would interest students and lead to meaningful discussions, movies with timeless universal themes, like *Breaking Away, Stand and Deliver, The Shawshank Redemption,* and *Gandhi.* My lack of sensitivity came to light after one of our film showings.

A couple male students came to my office a few days later, concern spread on their faces. "We need to talk with you," one of them announced.

"What is it?" I asked, not knowing what was on their minds.

"Why did you show us a movie like that? It offended us," the spokesman said.

"Which movie do you mean?" I inquired.

"*The Witness*," he replied. "According to our religion, we must not see a woman without clothing."

In that moment, I remembered the Amish woman taking a sponge bath while Harrison Ford caught a glimpse of her naked body. "I am so sorry," I stammered. "I forgot about that scene in the movie. Thank you for coming to tell me about it. In the future, we will be more careful. I'm sorry."

Nudity may have been taboo for my students, but smoking, in the culture, was not. Inside all AAUP buildings, however, smoking *was* prohibited. Waleed believed that it was appropriate to have a clean atmosphere, where non-smokers did not have to inhale second-hand smoke. The *No Smoking* signs were written in both Arabic and English, like all signs at the university.

I saw how unusual the idea was in Palestine when I attended meetings in high schools or at the Ministry of Education. Lighting up in the middle of a formal meeting was common. No one ever asked me if I minded. If there was no ashtray, the ashes were flicked either onto the floor or into an empty coffee cup on the table. When visitors came to the university unaware of the no-smoking policy, they puffed away as they walked around, dropping ashes on the floor.

It took time to persuade students that this was a bona fide policy that would be enforced. I became one of the self-declared smoking police during the early months of the first year. The dialogue was always the same between me and the male students who were smoking: "There's no smoking in the university," I stated, pointing at the sign as the student inhaled the favored LM brand.

"I'll just finish this cigarette," the smoker replied.

"No, you need to put it out right now," I answered back.

If the smoker thought I was kidding, I reached toward the cigarette in his mouth, ready to remove it myself. That usually moved the student to action, and he put out the cigarette in the nearest potted plant or wastebasket.

The entrance lobby had high ceilings and huge exterior walls of glass. Students sauntered around there with unlit cigarettes hanging between their lips, lighters in hand. They were either prepared for lighting up when they stepped outside, or they were testing me.

"I'm not against your smoking," I tried to convince them. "I just want everyone to follow the university policy." They did not believe me, but with time, students began to respect the rule.

We had a lot to learn from each other.

6

A Cold Night Outside

"Why do you want to teach here? Why don't you get a job in another country?" the Israeli army officer asked me one steamy afternoon as I sat in his air-conditioned cubicle at the army base.

"I love my job. I love my students," I said with conviction.

"But you know it's dangerous. You know they are against Israel. You should be careful."

"I feel completely safe," I smiled. "The people I work with are warm and friendly and invite me to their homes."

"Well, if you ever feel afraid, you have my number," the officer stated finally before we went on to discuss the current state of affairs.

Each semester I met with the Israeli army officer responsible for internationals working in the Jenin district. I visited the DCO, the Israeli District Coordination and Liaison Office, taking a list of the international faculty that semester, along with their passport information. The purpose of my visits was to keep updated about regulations and procedures, ensure that the DCO had the data needed to assist with problems at checkpoints, and build relationships.

Over time, I interacted with half a dozen officers, whose names and personalities became familiar to me. Not every officer lectured me on the risks of living in the West Bank. Some wanted to help the international teachers move through checkpoints as smoothly as possible.

"Checkpoint soldiers are not supposed to be aggressive with internationals," a DCO officer asserted to me. But that did not guarantee ease of movement. If a teacher was prevented from entering the West Bank, the teacher called me, then I called the DCO, then the DCO officer called the checkpoint soldier telling him or her to allow the teacher to pass.

This system was *not* in place, however, in the early days.

On a Thursday in mid-November 2000, my first year at the university, a Palestinian taxi driver from Jenin had agreed to pick Bob and me up in the nearby Israeli city of Afula at 9:00 in the evening. When the driver did not show at 9:00 or 9:30 p.m., I gave him a call to see what was going on.

"The roads are closed," he shouted into the phone. "Somebody got shot in Jenin today, so the Israelis closed the roads. I'm sorry. I cannot come to Afula to get you."

The news of another shooting disturbed me but did not surprise me. With my date book record of the number dead, I felt down as the numbers went up.

"Now what do we do?" Bob and I looked at each other, trying not to panic. It was long ago dark, and we were twelve miles from home, on the Israeli side of a checkpoint at Jalameh, a main point of entry into the northern West Bank.

In the fall of 2000, Palestinian drivers from Jenin were still able to pass through checkpoints and into Israel provided they had the proper permits. That morning, we had taken a taxi into the closest Israeli city of Afula, about twelve miles north of Jenin. We were curious to see what this nearby city was like, and I was eager to get cotton bed sheets since the sheets we had been provided with felt like sandpaper. The large, developed fields we passed that morning in Israel, with expansive irrigation systems and modern machinery, were unlike the small farms of the West Bank. On the edge of Afula, we neared a contemporary apartment building painted in blue, green, yellow, and red that stood out in the desert terrain. Now, after 9:00 in the evening, we were trying to get out of this modernity and back to our simple life in Palestine.

We called another driver from the West Bank, whose name and number we had jotted down earlier just in case we might need it. He agreed to pick us up on his side—the Palestinian side—of Jalameh checkpoint. Fifteen minutes later, near 11:00 p.m., we reached the checkpoint, paid the Israeli taxi driver, and watched him turn his car around and head back to Afula. Out in the middle of nowhere, we approached the checkpoint with passports in hand, weighted down with shopping bags. I had found not only cotton sheets but also baking supplies and foods unavailable in Jenin: brown sugar, chocolate chips, quick oats, wheat flour, legumes, mushrooms, broccoli, sweet potatoes, celery, ginger, and parmesan cheese. All of this we were lugging with us. We had dressed for a hot day and were starting to feel cold.

We were happy to see Barakat, the Palestinian driver who had come to meet us, approaching the checkpoint from the other side. A middle-aged man, tall and robust, he looked like a cuddly bear from a distance.

Between Barakat and us stood a couple of Israeli soldiers at their station. They wore army green with their hair slicked back, the gun-toting guards in their twenties. Their bullet-proof vests provided warmth from the evening chill, but during the daytime, the armor must have been hot.

"How are you?" I asked the soldier in charge as I handed him our passports.

"I'm OK," he replied, adjusting the rifle slung over his shoulder while he flipped through our passports. "Where are you going?" he asked, flipping away.

"We're going to the university. It's near Zababdeh. This is our taxi driver who is going to take us there," I responded, motioning to Barakat, who stood several feet away.

"I'm sorry, but you cannot go through," came his quick reply.

"But we have to. We live there," I said, anxiety lodged in my throat.

"I'm sorry, but there was a shooting today in Jenin, and it is not safe for you to go in. We have to do this for your own protection," the soldier patronized.

"But it's safe at the university, and our apartments are there," I protested. But to no avail.

Barakat then took his turn to appeal as he stepped closer to the soldier, Bob, and me. "I'm from that village over there," he said, pointing with his large hand towards his village a mile away. "They can come home with me and sleep in my house," he went on, putting his hand to his chest. "In the morning I can take them to the university." Barakat spoke in a soft and gentle manner. Is that his nature? I wondered. Or does he know that antagonizing a soldier will get him nowhere? I saw that night how Israeli soldiers tried to keep Palestinians in their place, and it sickened me.

"I'm sorry, but we cannot let them go in," the soldier directed at Barakat. We have our orders."

"Can I speak to whoever gives you your orders?" I inquired, keeping my cool. "Can you check with your commanding officer and explain our situation?"

The soldiers on duty agreed to call an officer of higher rank. It took some time, while Barakat, Bob, and I stood waiting in the November chill, wondering what would happen. A jeep roared up out of nowhere and came to a quick halt. Several officers jumped out, and we heard a thud as their boots hit the ground. "Good evening," one of them said. Then we had the same conversation all over again—my pleas, Barakat's attempts to convince the officer he would take care of us, and the officer's apologies as he refused to let us pass.

Up to this point, Bob had been mostly quiet, letting me take charge. Bob was naturally reserved, cautious, and non-confrontational, so he was happy to let me do the talking. I was surprised to suddenly hear him ready to defy their orders: "What will you do if we just walk through? Will you arrest us? Will you shoot us?"

"Is that what you think?" the soldier remarked as he leaned into Bob's face.

"We're just trying to get home," Bob softened.

"I will say again that you are not allowed to go through. I am very sorry."

We understood at that moment that there was nothing more we could do. We turned to Barakat, thanked him, and shook hands over the invisible line that we were not permitted to cross. We watched Barakat turn and amble away. Bob and I called him our Gentle Giant. We would remember how kind he had been to stand out in the cold for an hour, pleading on our behalf in his tender manner, offering his home to two strangers. He was the first of many angels who would pass through our lives in the years to come.

Bob and I turned around and tried to find a place out of the wind, sitting on some large gray rocks by the side of the road. It was midnight, and the temperature had dropped to about fifty degrees. A nearby metal sign rocked back and forth with a squeak. "Sounds like a horror movie," Bob joked. The chill started to move inside us, our fingers and toes going numb. Bob was in typical

Bob garb—a pair of jeans, a short-sleeved T-shirt, and Teva sandals. I had a windbreaker and was wearing socks and sneakers.

"We can't stay here all night. We'll freeze to death," I announced.

With a sliver of a moon and one yellow streetlight, the outlines of minarets and square houses of a village to our east were barely visible in the black sky. Another village to our west lay concealed down over a hill. We could have walked to either of those Palestinian villages within Israel, named Sandala and Muqableh, and someone might have offered us a place to stay. But at the time, we were novices in Palestine and did not realize the extent of Palestinian hospitality. We did not know how to call a taxi from Afula or directory assistance, and we had no emergency phone numbers with us. Later, Waleed reprimanded me for not calling him, but I did not feel I knew him or anyone else well enough to call so late. In retrospect, we were not very resourceful, but we tried to be.

"Maybe the soldiers can get us a taxi out of here," I told Bob. "I'm going to go ask them." I did not know where the taxi would take us but thought we would be able to find a hotel somewhere.

"We don't have any numbers," the soldiers replied, of no help.

"How about the police?" I suggested. The police will have to help us out, I thought.

"The checkpoint is out of our jurisdiction," a police officer on the other end of the line told the soldier who agreed to call on our behalf.

"What?" I asked, disbelief shaking my voice. How could a police officer refuse to assist someone in need? I wondered.

At around 1:00 in the morning, I sat down in the middle of the road, leaning up against the three-foot high cement barrier near the soldiers' cubicle. Bob stayed where he was, under a tree near the road. I wanted the soldiers to see me sulk, hoping to garner some sympathy. A while later, a soldier did bring us two wool army blankets. "Give them back before you leave," he said without emotion. The other soldiers seemed not to care.

By 3:00 a.m., Bob had joined me at the barrier, and the same soldier brought instant soup, tea, and a snack cake wrapped in plastic. We mumbled a thank-you as he set the tray down on the ground. I felt like a prisoner accepting food from my captor. Am I going to eat this? I wondered. Yet I soon gripped the hot cup of soup and held it between my hands, letting it warm my fingers. I drank, and it soothed my throat as well.

After this snack in the dark of night, Bob and I headed down the road, trying to stay warm. We considered moving through the field alongside the checkpoint, but we had no flashlights to lighten the way on the rocky unstable ground. We also feared what the soldiers might do.

Not far down the road we came to a cement structure with a dilapidated stone bench inside. This is excellent, we thought, as if we had found a hidden treasure. "We'll stay here till someone passes, and they can help us out," we said. "Maybe we'll be warmer, too." The wind was not as harsh inside the old bus stop, but the chill of the bench soon seeped into our bones.

Though it was the middle of the night, we were confident we would get a ride. When headlights approached from the road going towards Afula or the road leading to one of the Palestinian villages in Israel, we jumped up off the bench to wave down the driver. Each driver passed us by, however, like the priest and the Levite in Jesus' story of the Good Samaritan. Bob and I promised ourselves during the next few hours that we would never again pass by a person in need.

Our appearance did not help our case. Having torn open the package of bedsheets, we wore sheets draped around our bodies and pillowcases wrapped on our heads like turbans. Bob had folded a pillowcase over each foot inside his sandals.

"You look like a ghost," I teased.

"You do too," he teased back. He had a sense of humor even when he felt down.

I thought back to the first time I had met Bob. It was in the Nablus hotel where we stayed till our apartments were ready. The sound of his flute lured me to his door. When he answered my knock, there he was in the August heat, clad in a sheet as a toga. What's with the sheet? I wondered.

Now, in the November cold with sheets around us, we dozed on and off, half asleep in the broken-down bus stop, watching for cars and waiting for the sun to rise. We chuckled, and we whimpered. We prayed in our own ways—God, please help us.

At 6:00 in the morning, our prayers were answered. A Palestinian bus driver from the Arab Israeli village of Muqableh stopped his bus and looked at us questioningly. After listening to my explanation in limited Arabic, he assured us that he would help us get home.

We stepped onto the bus and fell into the front seats. I was sleepy and disoriented but could tell we were not heading in the direction of the university. Instead, we were going to Nazareth, where the driver had a daily bus route, picking up school children at home and delivering them to their school. For the next two hours, we slept on and off as our bodies thawed out with the soothing heat of the bus. School kids got on, joking with their friends. I forced my eyelids open occasionally to look at them.

After the bus route was finished, the driver took us to his village home, offered us coffee, and gave us a chance to wake up. It was 9:00 a.m., about twenty-four hours after we had left our own homes. We learned that the driver's name was Saeed, but we thought of him as our road angel, our second angel of the night.

Saeed was a young man, not more than thirty, clean-shaven with a cheerful smile. Inside his home, Saeed's parents were sitting on a thin foam mattress on the tile floor. While Saeed related to them what had happened to us, his mother offered us coffee. She poured the dark roast from a thermos on the low table into demitasse cups with blue, calligraphic designs. She and Saeed's father conversed back and forth, commenting on the roadblocks and *Al-Wade'*, The Situation. *"Shu hanamil? Kul min Allah,"* she repeated several times, lifting her hands in a questioning gesture. "What can we do? Everything is from God."

Her words imprinted themselves in my mind. Saeed's mother recognized God in her life, no matter what happened. I would meet many like her in Palestine who, no matter what, would say, *"Alhamdullilah,"* meaning "Thank God."

Saeed asked if we were ready to go, and we said yes, eager to get home. We thanked his parents for their hospitality and graciously accepted their gifts. Muslim prayer beads and a flask of perfumed oil were traditional gifts given by those returning from the *hajj*, the pilgrimage to Mecca.

Saeed drove us in his car through farm fields on a journey like none I had ever experienced. Jalameh checkpoint was still closed, as were the main roads, so the only way to get to the university was by off-road driving, which meant driving on dirt roads or through fields. The Mercedes station wagon, a popular choice in the region, bounced around over the rocky ground. The barley and wheat in the fields were both just beginning to grow. I did not know where we were exactly but trusted that Saeed did.

An hour later, close to noon by my watch, we pulled up in front of our apartment building at the university. "Thank you so much," we said to Saeed. "We don't know how to thank you enough."

Saeed shook our hands, "No problem." We took our shopping bags and headed upstairs to our respective apartments. Our nightmare was finally over.

I tried in vain all day to get warm, sitting in a living room chair in my flannel pajamas under a fuzzy acrylic blanket. The next day was Saturday, the first day of the work week at school. But I stayed in my pajamas and asked friends to cover my classes. I could not imagine going back to my office or the classroom after what I had experienced. Questions filled my mind: How could life proceed as normal? How do people cope in this situation? What is important in life, and what is not? What matters to me, and what does not?

After two days of introspection, Waleed came over to see me. As I was telling him my story, he kept saying, "I can't believe it." Of all the colleagues who called or stopped by, Waleed seemed the most sympathetic.

Then he said, "You have to get up and get dressed! Why don't you drive my car to Zababdeh and get some food? It would be good for you."

I appreciated the fact that our university president drove a worn-out vehicle whose air conditioning did not work, so when he enticed me with his old BMW, it worked. I drove to and from Zababdeh that evening, made myself eggs and potatoes for dinner, and returned to work the next day, feeling more like myself.

At the end of the week, I invited my students over to my apartment during each class hour. Bob had helped me make enough apple crisp for the three groups of twenty, and I served tea as well. Though the apple crisp was not a big hit, my students did appreciate the story I shared with them about my experience outside in the night.

I gained hero status that day. As my students said, "Now you know how we feel." To a certain extent, I did. I could empathize with a student who had spent months in prison sitting on cold, hard cement. My own head ached for five days after leaning against that cold cement bus stop wall. I could relate to students held up by Israeli border guards on their way to class. I would no longer expect those who had trouble coming to campus to quickly bounce back into classroom life.

A few days later, I got a card from a female student named Dunia:

> *Hi teacher, I wish you are better now after what happened to you in Afula. I don't know why I find myself holding this pen and writing to you, but your story affected me a lot and I wanted to express that to you and to let you know that we all feel with you. Teacher, a lot of things happens to all of us, but you must just let it pass. I know it affected you a lot, but I am sure that now you know how we Palestinians live and what we suffer. I don't know what to write next except take care of yourself. I love you, my sweetest teacher.*

I also got offers from students to learn more about their faith. "Islam," one student said, "can help you after your difficult experience." For most of my Muslim students, converting me to Islam was not a priority, but I appreciated their expression of care.

If everything in life is a lesson, then the lesson I gained was one of understanding. I wrote in my journal: *Maybe I went through this to feel a glimpse of the hatred that my students feel so that I will stop judging.* Prior to the night outside, when students bombarded me with their rhetoric, "You see what the Jewish do to us? You see how they treat us," I felt impatient at times, even while trying to be a good listener. I thought they could be more loving, less hateful, more peaceful, less violent in their responses. A week earlier, I had written in a letter to friends and family back home, *My heart hurts when I think that Palestinian kids are being taught to hate Jews, and Jewish kids are being taught to hate Palestinians.*

In my Mennonite childhood, I learned that hate, violence, and war were wrong. I believe in the teachings of Jesus: to love my enemies, pray for those who persecute me, turn the other cheek, and go the second mile. Because of my pacifist beliefs, I had little tolerance when I first lived in Palestine for the expression of anything but peace.

While these convictions did not change due to my encounter, the night outside helped me understand and accept my students' feelings. When they are victimized, I will not disregard their emotions, I resolved. I will try to refrain from judgment.

If every cloud has a silver lining, mine was the bond I felt with Bob after the experience we had endured. He was the person I wanted to be with following the incident. He was the one who understood. Neither of us knew it at the time, but we would become bonded for life.

7

Wandering the Hills

The university lay nestled in limestone hills. Bushes grew in the rugged terrain along with olive, almond, and cypress trees. Small villages speckled the hills and were visible from my apartment.

To the south, the tiny village of Talfit stood atop a low hill, home to about ten families. In the makeshift mosque standing near a high stone arch of a rundown, ancient ruin, Muslim men from the village and the university gathered each Friday for prayers.

Talfit was home to Hisham, a friendly farmer. The heavy wrinkles lining his face made him older than his fifty years. In addition to tending the landowner's olive trees, Hisham raised turkeys, chickens, and goats. He often brought fresh eggs, cheese, olives, and olive oil to Waleed. When I saw Hisham with his animals, I thought of my father, who had worked for a turkey company in his younger years. Dad would enjoy seeing these turkeys, I thought.

Hisham had a lot of children; the youngest few ran around the village in bare feet. The oldest, Murad, got a job as a doorkeeper for our apartment building after dropping out of junior high school. Once the university opened, Hisham took a day job as a security guard.

Palestinian villagers, many of whom were farmers, got jobs at the university in the hopes of improving their economies. The university changed their lives as they became security guards, groundskeepers, maintenance workers, photocopiers, mail clerks, and custodians. *"Sabah al-khayr,"* I greeted Hisham good morning as I arrived each day on campus.

To the north, a few houses made up the village of Tanin, which the Israeli army would turn upside down in the future in their search for men on their wanted list. Smaller than Talfit and with no electric power, the life of the village coincided with the rising and setting of the sun. On my early-morning walks, between 5:30 and 6:00, I saw a herd of sheep and goats in the hills along with their shepherd and sometimes a cow or two. When a village cow died, it was thrown into an old, unused well nearby, and for weeks after, I held my nose walking past.

To the west, a blanket of magenta and orange spread over the hills as the sun set each evening. Lateef, a shepherd, lived to the west in the winter months. I first met Lateef one day while out walking with Bob. "Hey, America!" shouted a man from a ridge up above us.

Lateef lived with his wife, Fareeda, and their five young children in a tent near our home. Lateef had piercing blue eyes and an exuberant smile shining through the scruffy whiskers on his thin face. Fareeda's huge brown eyes glistened like her white teeth. They lived in an open field during the summer and moved to a valley protecting them from the strong western winds in the winter. Lateef called their homes Summerland and Winterland.

Lateef and his family welcomed Bob and me inside their winter abode one day when we were out walking. When it began to rain, we stayed dry and warm inside the large canvas tent. Fareeda served tea with sprigs of *marameyya*, or sage, warmed on an open fire made from gathered twigs.

Lateef, what a character! His phenomenal mastery of English came from listening to BBC on his battery-powered radio. With an avid interest in history, politics, and popular culture, he named two of his daughters after well-known American women. Lateef loved to talk and would hold anyone crossing his path captive.

His eyesight was twenty-twenty. "Bob! Bob!" echoed in the distance when Bob and I were out walking. We could not see anyone, but we knew it was Lateef, beckoning us to another rousing conversation.

He began many of his exclamations with "Belief me," while thumping his fist to his chest. He repeated his political diatribes: "Do you know Apache? Why do Americans kill Red Indians and then name their weapons, like Apache helicopter, after them?"

Shepherding provided a steady source of income that kept Lateef self-sufficient. His college education had been interrupted in the late 1980s by the first intifada. He, like many Palestinian teenaged boys and young men, had been arrested for throwing stones and had then spent time in prison. His life course had changed, but he enjoyed the freedom of the shepherding life. His sharp mind became even sharper since he spent all day thinking.

Lateef preserved a traditional way of life that felt close to the earth. In Palestine, I could not help but appreciate people's affection for their land.

Bob was a wanderer like me. He took his walks in the late afternoon after the kids left school. From my apartment, I heard his footsteps shuffling up the stairs as he returned from his walks. On the weekends, we would walk together, sometimes with other teachers. "*Yalla!* Let's go!" we said, with an Arabic word that we used every day.

With countryside all around, there was plenty of ground to explore, except in winter when the rains turned the red earth to mud.

Hillside caves and a lone hot spring called us in. We hummed, and then sang, *I've been through the desert on a horse with no name.*

"Look at that stone," I exclaimed.

"Look at that bush," Bob retorted, beginning a game of one-upmanship we enjoyed.

Slabs of rock made great spots for picnics or naps. The sun warmed us when the weather was cool, and we sought shade when it sweltered. We listened to the silence, or the bleating of the sheep going home at sundown. Watching the hawks overhead made us giddy. One evening, we saw two pygmy owls, so tiny and cute, on a tree branch.

"Where can he be?" Bob asked about the wildcat he had once seen blending into the landscape.

"Are you sure that's what you saw?" I doubted.

"Nobody believes me," he answered.

On our hikes, we picked up fossils, bones, ancient stones, and pottery shards, starting a collection of treasures. In a nearby pine forest, we found a porcupine quill and saw mating box turtles.

The terrain we hiked was rocky. Limestone boulders penetrated the turf; smaller rocks were scattered. Herbs like sage and thyme grew wild, as did wild onions. But little green appeared except in spring. *No wonder the sheep are so scrawny,* I thought. *What do they find to eat?*

We discovered the popular *khubezeh,* or mallow. Having seen it in the local market, we assumed it was a tasty treat. Waleed taught us how to chop up the emerald leaves, fry them in olive oil with a bit of onion, sprinkle them with lemon and hot pepper sauce, and eat them with pita bread. A vegetarian who ate simply, Waleed was also an expert at *mujadara,* a Middle Eastern classic of rice, lentils, and onions. Not only university president, but cooking guide.

As Bob and I foraged for herbs, children sometimes appeared out of nowhere shouting, "What's your name?" in English at the top of their lungs. One time, we asked them to point out the edible plants. When they led us to a plant with dark leaves, we collected a small stack in our hands. The children said we could either sauté the leaves or roll them with rice inside. We decided to sauté them and did so in Bob's apartment. What the children had failed to mention was that we must first soak and boil the leaves several times before sauteing them, to rid them of their bitter juices.

"Let's try it at the same time," Bob and I agreed. Then "Oh no," we both groaned. We spit out the horrid greens into the kitchen sink and gripped our throats, which seemed to be swelling. "Was it poison?" we gasped.

After a while, "*Alhamdulillah*" came from our lips. Thank God we would have more days ahead to wander the hills.

8

Being a Foreigner in Jenin

"Do you face hostility from your students because you are an American?" asked the interviewee on the other end of the telephone line. I heard that question repeatedly during spring semester as I interviewed potential teachers for the following year.

"There *is* anti-American sentiment on campus," I replied, "but most students are learning to distinguish between the American government and American citizens like myself."

Making that distinction between my government and me did not come naturally for everyone at first, not for students at the university nor for people in town. Jenin was not a spot on the tourist track and had not attracted a lot of *ajaaneb,* or foreigners, in the past. When our group arrived in the fall, we seemed to be a novelty.

We were about a dozen individuals of varying ages and backgrounds, half single, mostly American, all new to Palestine. Two Mormon couples from Utah, including Jim and his wife and a family with children, worked on campus but lived in Zababdeh. In the same town, a young Presbyterian couple worked with the Latin Patriarchate school. We all became a group of friends.

In a shop on the lively streets of Jenin, I heard, "Look what America is doing to Palestine! You see what Bush is doing to us! You should tell Bush to stop what he is doing! You should tell people in your country what you see!" And I had just stepped into a drug store to buy shampoo!

Going to Jenin made the weekend. Teachers often rode the eight miles together in a shared taxi or minivan. Earth-colored, stone houses lined the roads that we drove on. Shops with red, green, or yellow awnings and metal doors edged the streets that we walked on.

Except when Israeli soldiers, *jaysh* in Arabic, came and closed things down, Jenin was a bustling place. People walked in all directions, men hand in hand with men, women with women, just like our students at the university. Many men and women wore head coverings. Women toted children and shopping bags. Chatter and laughter filled the air along with the call to prayer, car engines running, horns honking, and vendors shouting in the open-air market. *"Shekleen shekleen,"* vendors called out. Two shekels (about fifty cents) for a kilo of oranges or apples stacked like pyramids on carts. At the taxi stand, amber minivans and eight-person cars waited to fill up.

Stopping at a food stall was a must, I thought. *Falafel* sandwiches, made of fried ground chickpeas in a pocket bread, came laden with crunchy cucumbers, greasy fried eggplant, and pink pickled turnips. They dripped with *tahini,* made from sesame seeds.

Besides eating, I was also fond of shopping. In the rug shop, a burgundy carpet for my living room called out to me. The wicker store provided a hall tree, bookshelf, and stools. In the plastics shop, I bought wash tubs, storage bins, and clothes hangers. The kitchen store supplied me with speckled melamine bowls from China and the tiny aluminum plates I loved to collect. But the clothing store was not for me. I'm glad I brought what I needed from the States, I thought, seeing what Jenin had to offer. My casual wardrobe suited me fine.

Bob and I never tired of the market. "Look at all these cucumbers I got for one shekel," I exclaimed.

Bob answered back, "Look at these tomatoes I got for about twenty-five cents!" He bought a box to make salsa.

Palestinians strolling in the streets greeted us with "Hello" or with the Arabic *"Marhaba."* Some said, *"Salam alaykum,"* a typical Arabic greeting. The response to *"Salam alaykum,"* meaning "Peace be upon you," was *"Wa alaykum as-salam,"* meaning "And unto you, peace." It was like passing the peace in church, I thought.

Shopkeepers greeted us with *"Itfaddalu." Itfaddalu* meant "Welcome. Please come in. Please join me for coffee." I sipped many cups of coffee with people I had just met on Thursday mornings in Jenin. With that kind of warmth, it was hard to take offense at people's outbursts about America. I agreed with their sentiments anyway, so I could join in, explaining my disapproval of American policy in the Middle East.

In time, the tirades softened as people in Jenin became accustomed to having *ajaaneb* around. They began to see that we foreigners supported the Palestinian people. When somebody inquired, "Where are you from?" and I responded, "America," the next question—"You like Bush?"—was meant more as a greeting than a question requiring a reply, in the same way that "How are you?" is used as a greeting in the U.S. Instead of asking me if I liked Bush, some people just said, "George Bush! He's crazy!"

When I spoke Arabic to people in Jenin, they were just as interested in asking me, "Which is better: Egypt or Palestine?" My Egyptian dialect gave me away. I first learned Arabic in Egypt, where I had volunteered with the Mennonite Central Committee, lived in a Coptic Orthodox convent, and taught English for three years after college. Expressions like *How are you? What's your name?* and *What do you want?* differed in the Egyptian and Palestinian dialects. As soon as I opened my mouth, the response was "Oh, you learned Arabic in Egypt!"

"Yes, I did," I smiled, wondering if I would ever speak like a Palestinian.

"Which is better: Palestine or Egypt?"

"Every country is good," I declared, "but I like Palestine very much. The land is *beautiful*, and the people are *kind* and *friendly*," I said, emphasizing each adjective. Palestinians were always striking up conversations.

Sometimes, Arabic speakers talked *about* me instead of *with* me, unaware that I understood Arabic. In a taxi one day, I listened to a conversation between a passenger and the driver.

"Where is she from?"

"America."

"What does she do?"

"She works at the university."

"Is she a doctor?" (meaning "*Does she have a doctorate?*")

"I think so."

"Is she married?"

"I don't know."

At the university, students from Jenin mimicked what I heard in town: "Which is better: Palestine or America? You see what America is doing to us! Is it fair?" If only my students could understand that I did not agree with my government's policies, I thought. If only they knew that Bob and I sat on the sofa one day, calculating what three billion dollars in annual U.S. aid to Israel meant per capita. All those zeros confused us.

I knew that life was unfair to my students, and I knew that they needed an outlet to express their feelings. I wanted to be that outlet, having learned that my role was to listen, and having vowed not to judge. But sometimes, it was difficult.

At times, I felt accosted. I could not walk through the hall to my office without a student confronting me about America. The accusations were usually directed at the U.S. government or Israel, at George Bush or Ariel Sharon, not at me. In any case, I felt tired. I took off my glasses and rubbed my nose or massaged my growing headache. Sometimes, I put my head on my desk and rested for a moment.

A few students accused us international teachers of being CIA agents or of collaborating with Israeli intelligence, but those charges were rare. We usually heard *about* them rather than hearing them ourselves.

My students generally charmed me with their curiosity and bright sense of humor. I usually walked out of class invigorated.

Abeer, a studious young woman with radiant eyes, said to me one morning after class, "That was a good class today." I appreciated her comment since female students seemed a bit less interactive outside of class.

One of my many Muhammads, a distinguished-looking guy, said to me in the hall one afternoon, "Thank you for teaching us, Miss Cynthia. Thank you for being patient with us even when we're lazy and don't do our homework."

Anas, an artistic student with shoulder-length hair, a rarity for males at AAUP, stopped in my office one day. "Hi, Miss Cynthia," he began.

"Hi, Anas. How are you?" I inquired.

"I'm fine, thanks God. I wanted to bring you something for your birthday." Earlier that week, I had worn a T-shirt to class touting *Over the Hill* on the front, a family piece passed down from my older sister to my older brother to me. I announced to my students, "Yesterday was my birthday. How old do you think I am?"

Their response, "forty-five," shocked me. I had just turned forty but had always thought of myself as young-looking. I had energy and very few gray hairs, though my shoulders were starting to curve. I was only slightly fashionable, but my clothes were not outdated either. Yet I realized my students saw me as older than their own mothers.

Anas handed me a pencil drawing of two rams, one facing front drawn in black and the other facing to the side drawn in red. He had written my birth date and had signed it. "Oh, that's beautiful," I said, pleased with my first gift. "You are a talented artist. Thank you."

"I also have this for you," he said, giving me a dark blue mug with a ram and *Aries* printed in gold lettering.

"Oh, I like it too much," I exclaimed, using an expression my students used. I then asked Anas about his own sign of the zodiac. The zodiac mugs would spruce up the desks of many of my colleagues as their popularity grew. I did not know then that I would receive lots of memorable gifts in the future.

Not only our students but also AAUP faculty and staff, for the most part, welcomed us. They treated us as fellow professionals and members of the academic community. The faculty was a small group of about twenty at the beginning, and we got together throughout the year. Palestinian instructors of biology, chemistry, mathematics, sociology, accounting, and law, many of whom had lived and been educated abroad, met with us teachers of English to discuss the language needs of our students and ways we could collaborate.

The registrar and I had a shared understanding of how to handle student issues that arose. We spent hours together each semester. No matter how much work there was to do, if I was in the registrar's office mid to late morning, he invited me to join his team, which included my friend Nabeela, for a quick breakfast break. Sitting around a small table, telling new jokes, we shared a common plate of bread, olives, soft white cheese, and *hummus,* the popular chickpea dip. I could catch my breath in the registrar's office.

During the midyear break between semesters in February, I offered English classes for staff. Twenty-six people divided into three groups attended the two-week course, three days a week during their workday. We discussed a range of topics, including The Situation, medical ethics, technology, and culture. On Valentine's Day, the theme was love and marriage, and my colleagues said, "This is our tradition" as they described arranged marriage practices. The staff seemed pleased to practice their English, and I felt energized teaching my colleagues. The bonds that had formed with Palestinian coworkers my first weeks in August were strengthened during that midyear break.

The same month, I held a conversational English class for the Jenin community, one of the first continuing education courses offered at AAUP. Though class size was small, the atmosphere of trust and mutual respect held great significance. As an optometrist, a pharmacist, a bakery owner, two dentists, and several businessmen met together that month, we conversed about an array of issues, debating, laughing, and listening to one another. Despite the oppression of everyday life outside the classroom, we had a great time.

Against tremendous odds, the Palestinian people I knew continued their lives in the most resilient manner possible. When the roads between the university and Jenin were closed, they found alternate routes of off-road driving, making new paths wherever they could. When not permitted outside their homes due to an Israeli curfew, people returned to work as soon as the curfew was lifted. The more I interacted with Palestinian people, the more I learned of their resilience. I felt grateful for every opportunity.

Ghaleb was a Jenin businessman in the continuing education class and AAUP board member. He was close to my age, well fed by his wife, with a dimple on each cheek and a joke on his tongue. Ghaleb informed Waleed, "Cynthia teaches with her eyes. She makes me want to study at home and prepare for the next class." The feelings were mutual.

Rewarding moments, however, did not mean that life was without challenges. Waleed received occasional calls from the governing Palestinian National Authority security office, informing him of possible threats to Americans. They reported that men on the run from the Israeli army might possibly kidnap foreigners. The advice for foreigners was "Don't go to Jenin." Waleed and I discussed what we should do. The university, wanting to heed the advice of the Palestinian Authority without causing alarm, asked us to keep a low profile.

When the situation eased, a university security guard accompanied us on our Jenin trips until the threats had dissipated. After that, we were asked to call Fakhree, the head of security, to check in before traveling anywhere. I had always considered myself independent and able to accomplish anything I wanted. Needing to depend on others for something as simple as going to town was a humbling reminder that I was an outsider, a guest in the land.

In addition, the U.S. State Department issued occasional warnings about possible actions against Americans in the West Bank. The international teachers met in Waleed's apartment one evening to discuss what to do. Several teachers were thinking of leaving for a time, while others were not convinced.

"What good will it do to leave for a few days?" "What will we do if we leave?" "How long will we be gone?" "Will anything be different when we return?"

We discussed what to do, along with the threats, whenever the need arose. It was not in my nature to be afraid, and I did not want to leave, but I needed to take the worries of others seriously and not minimize their fears. Thus, I joined the difficult conversations.

Frequent gunfire within hearing distance from our campus apartments was hard to get used to. We heard not only gunfire but also helicopters, F-16 fighter jets, and the sonic booms that reverberated when fighter jets broke the sound barrier. These reminders of Israel's military might sometimes frightened, sometimes intimidated, but mostly annoyed me.

Not knowing was the most difficult thing to handle. Even before smart phones, if there was a checkpoint, if Israeli tanks were approaching Jenin, if there had been an "operation," the Palestinian word for suicide bombing, everyone knew in a flash. Everyone, that is, but us. Palestinians living in this tense setting of chaos and upheaval were always on their toes with a sixth sense of alert about them, waiting for the next piece of bad news. Yet the communication network often eluded my foreign friends and me. We sometimes found out about Israeli tanks rolling into Jenin, only eight miles away, from the BBC news, broadcast 6,000 miles from us.

This may have come as some assurance to our families back home, that we were far enough from Jenin to be safe from all that was going on there. But it felt strange to be so close yet so unaware. I wanted to be included in the network, to be part of what was going on. I recognized, however, that I was still an outsider, a person who could choose to leave if I wanted to. Most of the Palestinian people I knew did not have that option.

AAUP 2000

AAUP 2004

"Get Waleed's Signature"—Waleed and Cynthia

"Ask Jim"—Susan, Waleed, Cynthia, and Samah

A street in the neighboring town of Zababdeh

The Palestinian village of Anza

Hiking down Mt. Hureish, Jenin's tallest peak

Hiking near the village of Raba—Michelle and Cynthia

Hill wandering near the university

Flock of sheep near the university

A road into Jenin

Jenin market

YEAR TWO

If

If you visit life, you visit a very big book.
If you look in someone's eyes, you live in a secret world.
If you visit a library, you visit another world you can't imagine.
If you look in the night, you see a secret thing you didn't see before.
If you want to see agony, then you should visit Palestine.

—Student, Arab American University of Palestine

9

A New Year

After two months back in the States, I flew into Tel Aviv the last week of August 2001, eager for the new academic year.

"You got fat!" a Palestinian colleague remarked upon my return. Usually seen as thin, I had gained five pounds thanks to my mother's cinnamon rolls and cherry pie and goodies that others fed me. But I was taken aback to hear it put like that. I thought of the previous year when a friend said to me, "You look much better this week than last." I wondered what she meant, since I had been feeling fine.

Taking note of linguistic expressions and gaining insights into culture through language were hobbies. I was used to the standard direct questions in Arabic culture, like "Are you married?" "Do you have children?" and "How much do you take?" referring to salary. But "You got fat" was a new one.

Amal, the woman who cleaned my office, hurried in with a smile. *"Hamdillah as-salameh,"* she exclaimed, meaning "Thank God for your safety."

I jumped up from behind my desk, and we embraced with a kiss on each cheek. *"Allah ye salmik,"* I answered. "May God give you peace."

Amal wore a traditional village gown with little adornment and a scarf that hid most of her hair. I guessed we were about the same age. Amal asked about my family, and I asked about hers. We talked about the summer, and then moved on to The Situation in Palestine.

Amal quickly spotted the latest toy I had brought back for my collection, a set of colored magnetic blocks to move around. Every day, Amal picked up the objects on my desk to dust under them, humming as she did so. Scarab beetles made of soap stone meant protection for life in Egyptian culture. A stone with a fossil of a sand-dollar that I had found near the university was my prized paperweight. Amal seemed to take as much pride in the objects on my desk as I did. Seeing Amal again, I felt glad to be back.

Throughout the previous year, Amal had been a bright spot in my day. When I first met her, she asked with curiosity about the family photographs on my bulletin board, wanting to know who each person was. I introduced her to my parents, siblings, nieces, and nephews.

I looked forward to this academic year. Samah, my new administrative assistant, recently graduated from college, was sure to add life to the English Language Center with her bright eyes, big smile, and cheery voice. We would establish a language lab and hire another Palestinian staff member. Five new instructors from Canada, England, Scotland, and the United States were coming, females and males ranging in age from mid-twenties to mid-forties. My recruiting efforts in the summer had paid off.

Waleed, Jim, and I went to Nazareth to pick up the teachers with Waleed's BMW and Jim's Peugeot. I would witness the new teachers' spirit that very night. Nazareth, known as the Arab capital of Israel because so many Palestinians live there, lay thirty miles from AAUP. In between Nazareth and AAUP stood Jalameh checkpoint, where Bob and I had been kept outside in the cold the previous year.

We arrived at Jalameh around 8:00 p.m., having already picked up the teachers in Nazareth. The Israeli soldier on duty asked where we were headed, went to check with his officer, and returned, declaring, "You can't go in."

Jim tried to convince him otherwise: "We are not Israeli citizens, so we have the right to enter." Israelis were not allowed to enter the West Bank at Jalameh unless they had a special permit or were Palestinians with Israeli citizenship.

The soldier consulted with his commanding officer again and then came back. This time he said, "You can go through, but not your cars."

Jim again tried to negotiate, but to no avail. Prevented from bringing the cars into the West Bank, Waleed and Jim decided to spend the night in Nazareth and try to cross in the morning. The rest of us would walk through the checkpoint. Though it was risky for any Palestinian to be out driving at night, Waleed made several phone calls and found a Palestinian driver on the other side to come pick us up.

Eight of us—the five new teachers, one spouse, the driver, and I—needed to fit into a tiny Fiat Ono, a vehicle made for four people. Though we had just met, we became fast friends as we configured ourselves inside the car, two layers of bodies, one on top of the other, in both the front and back seats.

All was still in the Palestinian villages we drove through: Arrana, Deir Ghazali, Beit Qad, Deir Abu Da'if, Im Tut, and Jalqamus. Off-road driving took us on gravel and dirt paths, beside olive trees covered in dust. I later named that route Moonscape because the moon gave a silvery glow to the dusty roads and trees. Taking it all in, we didn't know whether to talk or keep quiet. We didn't know whether to laugh or cry. I could only imagine what was swirling around in the mind of each teacher: "What have I gotten myself into?" If they were shocked, they covered it with a good sense of humor: "We knew it was going to be an adventure!"

The teachers seemed in good spirits the next day at orientation and after. We tested hundreds of students, graded their exams, visited Jenin, and ventured to the beach in Haifa on the weekend.

Haifa in the early twentieth century was predominantly Arab. By the mid-1900s, it was a mix of Arabs and Jews and was also important to people of the Baha'i Faith. In 1948, many Arabs fled after the city was captured by a Jewish paramilitary organization. Waleed's parents and older siblings were among those who fled. Today, the city is mostly Jewish with a small population of Palestinian Arabs.

With its white sandy beaches on the Mediterranean Sea, Haifa was a far cry from the reality of life in the West Bank under Israeli military occupation.

If that reality had not sunk in for the new teachers on the night drive through Moonscape, it came to the foreground the following week. On Tuesday, ten people in Jenin died at the hand of the Israeli army, and about half that number were killed on Wednesday. No employees or students from Jenin could reach campus with the city under Israeli military curfew. The first day of classes was cancelled. The Situation, *Al-Wade'*, and all its horrors came rushing back into my mind.

While that was going on, something else had happened. On the same Tuesday that ten people were killed by Israeli soldiers in Jenin at the beginning of the new academic year, planes crashed into the World Trade Center in New York and the Pentagon in Washington. It was September eleventh.

On September eleventh, I came home from work early, around 3:30 p.m. That was 8:30 in the morning in New York. As soon as I walked into my apartment, my American neighbor knocked on my door. "Come see what's on BBC," she urged. For the next couple of hours, two other American teachers and I sat with my neighbor in her living room, glued to the TV screen.

I snapped out of my shock later that evening when my phone rang. It was my Palestinian friend from work, Leen. "Cynthia, is your family OK? I'm very sorry about what happened," she said. I could hear the distress in her voice.

"Thank you," I responded. "My family is fine. They don't live near New York or Washington."

"Alhamdulillah," she said. "Thank God. It's terrible what happened. I can't believe it."

"Neither can I," I muttered. "Neither can I."

After I hung up, the phone rang again, and then a couple more times. With a tragedy unfolding in Jenin that day, and a larger scale calamity unfolding in New York, Palestinian colleagues called me to find out if my family was alright and to offer their condolences. On TV I saw young Palestinian men in West Bank streets celebrating the U.S. attacks. I understood their opposition to the U.S. support for the Israeli military machine. I also knew that those Palestinian men did not represent the whole of Palestine. There were many Palestinians living in the U.S., and I assumed their relatives in Palestine would be concerned. My friends who called me reminded me that many, if not most, Palestinians were sorry, not celebrating.

As I watched the international news over the next few days, Israeli army tanks surrounded Jenin and completely sealed it off. Air and ground attacks occurred in the middle of the night for three nights. Fifteen Palestinians in Jenin were killed, and over one hundred were injured as Palestinians continued to resist the occupation and the Israeli army continued to attack them. The university was a wasteland because no one could get there. The tanks remained in Jenin for a week, but that story did not get much news coverage. The Israeli army seemed to be taking advantage of the situation in the United States. While the world was focused on New York and Washington, Israel could do as it pleased in Palestine with little notice from the outside world.

I didn't know what the school year would hold. I didn't know how often I would stand in solidarity with my Palestinian students and friends. Neither did I know what a heartbreaking year it would be, with one misfortune after another. I naively thought that things would get better. I didn't think they could get worse. My naivete is perhaps what kept me going when things got tough.

10

No Ink in Palestine

Enrollment at AAUP increased from 300 students the first year to 1,500 the second. The teachers and I set about our work in the English Language Center. Our mission was to help students become more fluent in English. We placed 600 students into levels and made class schedules. We managed problems with the photocopier or not having chalk in our classrooms. Our language lab opened. The growing faculty and staff from other departments continued to collaborate with us. The governor of Jenin invited us in a public display of hospitality. The teachers began studying Arabic in an informal class setting.

Throughout those weeks, *Al-Wade'* revealed itself again and again, reminding us what Palestinians living in the West Bank faced. Because of the Israeli occupation, some families were without work and could not pay tuition costs for their sons or daughters. Parents and students came to Waleed, describing their financial problems. Waleed spent a lot of time listening. He did not want anyone to be dismissed from their studies, knowing what young people roaming the streets could mean. He helped find assistance for as many as he could.

Faculty and staff routinely did not get paid on time. Without adequate tuition income, the university depended on outside support to pay our salaries. University donors had already contributed thirty million dollars to get the university up and running. Now, they were called on to assist in this time of need. Transferring money from outside donors was sometimes difficult due to complex procedures imposed by Israel following Palestinian attacks.

Even when the university transferred our salaries to the bank, that did not ensure it would be easy for us to get cash. One day, I spent three hours in the bank waiting for my number to come up. Jenin had just opened after ten days under Israeli curfew, and 220 people waited in line in front of me. Another time, the bank did not have enough cash. "Sorry," the teller said. "We don't have money today."

As the political situation worsened, Israel stopped delivering mail to the West Bank. Since Israel was in control of the borders, that meant no mail for months at a time. When mail did come, it was often received long after it had been sent. One time, I opened a Valentine's card that my younger sister had sent me twelve months earlier. Six letters from my ninety-six-year-old grandmother in Iowa, who wrote to me once a month, came all in one bundle. Sensitive to the need for reliable correspondence and with help from relatives in Nazareth, Waleed arranged for AAUP to share a post office box with an organization in Nazareth, where the postal services would not be interrupted.

Having a mailbox in Nazareth, however, did not guarantee that we would get letters and packages in a timely manner. We still had to get the mail from Nazareth, which involved transporting it from Israel to the occupied West Bank across the Jalameh checkpoint. I arranged ways for the mail to come or picked it up myself. Waleed also became a delivery person since he had an international passport and yellow plates on his car, signifying an Israeli vehicle.

Travel restrictions imposed by Israeli forces made it difficult to receive not only mail but also construction materials, university equipment, and academic supplies. In spite of the limitations, Waleed insisted that the university continue building new buildings and developing new academic programs.

Faculty and staff got to work despite checkpoint hardships. Samah described travel between Jenin and AAUP. In her well-fitted pants, stylish shirt, and complementary earrings, Samah pointed to her mud-caked shoes. "The soldiers forced us off the AAUP bus, and the road was muddy. Isn't that nice?" she laughed.

Another day she reported, "Today, we had to leave our vehicle and walk up and down the dirt path until we could find another car. You know that place, I think."

Each day Samah bounced into my office, sometimes with a tale to tell. Every hair was in place, and her smile showed her straight white teeth. Her exuberant, musical "Good morning" resounded.

Samah gave accounts of not only muddy shoes and pant legs but also humiliation. She spoke of her own experiences as well as what colleagues and students endured. On one occasion, a bus carrying university employees was ordered by a gruff soldier to pull over, and the passengers were commanded to get out and stand in the drizzling rain. After checking all their ID cards, instead of handing them back, the soldier threw the ID cards into a mud puddle.

In another instance, employees and students on their way home to Jenin were directed off the bus and made to wait over four hours before their ID cards were returned. They were forced to sit on the thorny ground, at first hot with the sun and later cold after the sun had gone down. They could not use their cell phones or relieve themselves for four hours.

When colleagues told their stories, a weight came upon me, and my words stuck in the back of my throat. I usually looked my friends in the eyes, heaved a sigh, and said simply, "I'm sorry."

My colleagues came back with "This is our life. What shall we do?" I heard "This is life" time and time again.

In mid-October 2001, we ran out of toner for our printer in the English Language Center. Samah was usually on top of things like that. We rarely ran out of anything after she joined the center.

"There's no ink in Palestine," she said when I asked if she had requested more toner.

"What do you mean, there's no ink?" I asked.

"There's no ink at any shops in the West Bank, not in Jenin or Nablus or Ramallah. Because of the Israeli curfews and closed roads, no shops can get ink from Israel. I'm sorry."

Unbelievable, I thought to myself. The Israeli occupation affects every aspect of life.

My students wrote how the occupation, the intifada, and the Israeli response to the intifada affected their lives:

Dear Human Being, How can a person describe feelings of pain? How can we find a way to show others how much the Palestinian people are suffering? Whatever we say and however we say it, we cannot give this issue its rights. Human being, imagine that you lost your nationality, name, home, freedom, and rights. Just like a bird whose wings were cut by a bad man. This bad man stole the bird's life because he left him alive. But what a life filled with suffering! This is our story of the occupation.

One of the dangerous effects of the Israeli response to the intifada is unemployment. Statistics show that the greatest economic decline and unemployment rate is in Jenin; 90 percent of the overall laborers in the city are without work. The Palestinians who were working in Israel lost their jobs because they cannot reach their workplace due to the closure that the Israeli government imposed on the Palestinian regions. In addition, the bad situation prevents Arab people in Israel from coming and buying goods from the Palestinian markets; this affects the local market very much. To put an end to this bad phenomenon, peace negotiations must go ahead and find a quick solution to this Arab-Israeli conflict.

There are many effects that resulted from the Israeli response to our intifada, one of which is the shortage of food in the cities of Palestine. This happens because of many reasons. First, Israel destroyed and damaged large areas of agricultural land with the yields and changed them to Jewish settlements or roads for soldiers. Second, the farmers in Palestine sometimes cannot go to their lands to plant them or take care of their plants. Third, Israel doesn't allow food aid to reach the cities. Fourth, some people in Palestine don't have money to buy food for their families. In summary, these effects came from the Israeli procedures to put the Palestinian people under its control.

Palestine has a large percentage of disabled people, which is an effect of Israeli's response to the intifada. First, Israeli soldiers aim at Palestinians in the upper part of the body, which causes handicaps. Research shows that in the first 25 days of Al-Aqsa Intifada, there were 207 disabled people, half of whom were disabled in the upper part of the body. Second, an ambulance takes a lot of time to reach the injured because of the roadblocks that Israelis put along the roads, so the patient's condition may become worse until the help comes to him or her. Third, Israelis forbid medicine and medical instruments from reaching Palestinian clinics. The political situation of the country has also forced a lot of qualified doctors to leave, so we don't have the right staff who can treat any case. In the end, I hope this situation ends without any new victims.

The things I take for granted in other places cannot be taken for granted here, I thought. What will be next? I wondered.

11

The Happy Van

Of the 476 dreams I recorded while in Palestine, 134 were about work. I dreamed about placement testing, student schedules, registration procedures, and class lists. Classroom reading materials laced with anthrax. Students that annoyed me and students I adored. Computers, printers, and photocopy machines. Office renovations, furniture, and painted walls. Apartments that weren't ready when teachers showed up, and teachers who left early. Teachers' performance, anxieties, relationships, children, hairstyles, and clothes. Suitcases packed and airport security inspections. I dreamed about trying to get Waleed's signature.

The dreams reflected what my daily life involved. Waleed once shared a proverb: *Life ends, but work never ends.* When I agreed to the post of English Language Center Director, no job description existed. I could not predict what my job or my life would entail. As for any administrator, unforeseen tasks came my way. Plus, the university was new, and the political situation was volatile.

Teachers were one of my big challenges. It was my job to find teachers, help them in their work, and keep them happy. Waleed had agreed with me from the first day that if teachers were not happy, they would not stay, and our experience had confirmed that.

Waleed and I jokingly referred to the faculty and staff with whom we worked as "my people" and "your people." He was responsible for many more people than I, and as he put it, "It takes some pressure off me knowing you'll take care of your people."

Keeping my people comfortable at home was key. "Cynthia, my apartment is flooded!" "Cynthia, we don't have water!" "Cynthia, there's no hot water in our apartment!" Teachers called me day and night. I then called the head of maintenance, Sulaiman.

"I'll take care of it," Sulaiman replied each time. His calm demeanor served him well with the unending tasks required of him as new buildings went up and needed to be maintained. He never seemed to lose his cool, and he spoke to his staff with respect. If I were a local villager looking for a job, I would want to work with Sulaiman, I thought.

Cockroaches took over several apartments. I opened the door to show a new teacher her apartment and found roaches scurrying across the living room floor. Not a few, but tens. The teacher, with her black braided hair and dark eyes, exclaimed, "Cockroaches! I've never seen so many cockroaches in my life! I guess I'll be okay."

"I am so sorry," I stuttered. "I had no idea. I'll talk to our maintenance man first thing in the morning."

An influx of ants graced some apartments, while mosquitoes infested others. At work in the mornings, I got the latest mosquito report from teachers: "Last night we killed five before we went to sleep!"

Sometimes, it was neither water nor critters. "Cynthia, I can't sleep! It's 11:00 at night, and there's still construction going on outside." "Cynthia, the girls in the dorm below are keeping me awake!" "Cynthia, my cable TV is not working again!" We were grateful for the channels we had, even though most were Arabic stations. Every one of us had CNN in English, and some got BBC.

A teacher emailed me, *Cynthia, I am requesting an emergency meeting to discuss the failure of the university to pay the staff. I am concerned not only about myself but also about the Palestinian faculty and staff.* I invited the teacher to my office, along with Leen, my Palestinian friend on staff.

Posters of Palestine, a painting of Bob's, and books lined the walls of my office. Through the green metal-framed windows, the countryside was in sight.

As Leen walked in, I saw how comfortable she was in her long, flowing *jilbab*. She sat down at the conference table, along with the teacher and me. I shared the teacher's concern with Leen, who turned to him and said, "Don't worry about us. We are used to this. We know we will get paid sometime."

I usually kept my office door open. Teachers popped in, their patience wearing thin. "Cynthia, do you know when we'll be getting mail from Nazareth?"

"I wish I did," I said.

I informed teachers of whatever I knew as soon as I learned it. I felt like a dispatcher receiving and sending out information. Samah helped by translating emails that came to me in Arabic. When a challenge came my way, she looked at me with her knowing eyes. I looked back at her and said, "How did I manage for a whole year without you?"

When the news concerned the political situation, I updated teachers and listened to their concerns. Some wanted a contingency plan. They wanted to know how we would get out fast if the situation warranted it. Though I did not feel the same sense of urgency, I helped the group create a plan that satisfied their anxieties.

In our program, administrative details had been ironed out, and the English Language Center was running efficiently.

Computer and printer problems persisted, however. A teacher flew into a rage one day shouting, "How can I teach with no working printer?"

I thought back to the days when the university first opened and our center had no printer, no copy machine, no paper cutter, no secretary, no hot water, no cold drinking water, no toilet paper, no fans, no chalk, no white boards, no bulletin boards, no resources. We've come a long way, I thought.

My job would teach me a lot. I could not please everyone all the time. Others would blame me for their unhappiness. Working with people and all their idiosyncrasies was part of an administrator's life. This is life, I thought. This is my life—to accept and respect all my teachers.

I knew that life on the hill, as we had come to call it, was difficult. I also knew that I should draw the line between my professional and personal life. But when a teacher felt bad about something, I, in turn, felt bad. I lugged the problems home with me. What could I have done differently? How can I make things better now? As I tormented myself with thinking, self-doubts grew. Am I right for this job? I wondered.

I sometimes caught Waleed in his office in the late afternoon. "Tell me what's going on," he would say, giving me time to respond. When he saw my discouragement from behind his desk, he might say, "Let's go for a walk." Our brisk strides took us along the road that led to the university or into the surrounding hills. Waleed liked to pick the green almonds that Palestinians loved to eat, crunchy and with salt. We scavenged for wild cilantro, a treat not found in the local market. The walks helped clear my mind or gave me a fresh outlook.

Waleed decided that the university would provide the international faculty with a vehicle to share. I agreed that having access to four wheels might offer a break from the isolation and help alleviate frustrations. I was responsible for finding a van to buy, carrying four thousand dollars in cash to the seller, traveling a couple hours to Haifa to transfer the title, completing the required paperwork, taking the vehicle to Nazareth each year for inspection, and having the vehicle repaired when needed.

We named the 1991 VW Caravan the Happy Van. Blue on the bottom and white on the top, she took us on blissful trips, beginning with Camel Beach in Haifa. But the Happy Van became the Unhappy Van in less than a year. I had to resolve the conflicts that arose from a dozen or so people trying to share the vehicle.

I received a note under my apartment door from a teacher who had agreed to be in charge: *Dear Cynthia, I no longer want to be responsible for the Happy Van. There are too many conflicts among people. My job is already too stressful, and I don't get paid enough to have this added stress.* I felt like taking back all the keys and selling the van if teachers could not stop bickering.

Aside from the interpersonal conflicts, I received phone calls from teachers: "Cynthia, we've run out of gas and are stuck in the middle of nowhere!" "Cynthia, the Happy Van isn't working!" "Cynthia, we got stuck in the mud!" Once, the engine burned out and had to be replaced. One teacher hit a wall on a village street, while another ran a red light in Israel.

Fines in Israel were steep, as were penalties for not paying them. The forty dollars owed for a teacher's use of a toll road in Israel turned into a bill of two hundred fifty dollars. Each month that the bill remained unpaid, a higher penalty was added. But since we did not receive mail regularly, we knew nothing of the fine or mounting debt.

Sometimes, I was just so tired. Even with the Happy Van, I could not keep teachers happy.

Bob was in Mexico that year. He had returned to teach in San Miguel de Allende, an artist community where he had lived and worked for four years before going to Palestine. Though we communicated by email and Skype, I missed him. With Bob gone, I took up more of Waleed's time. One day I was telling Waleed how much I missed Bob. "I need Bob to be here," I said emphatically.

"No, *I* need Bob to be here," he smiled. Later the next summer, after my second year at AAUP, Bob and I would get married, and Waleed would get a break.

12

Visits to Jenin Refugee Camp

In early March 2002, I joined seventy AAUP students, faculty, and staff on my first visit to Jenin Refugee Camp. We went to the camp to see the damage from an Israeli military siege and to show our support for the people. We went to express our condolences to Khalil Suleiman's family.

Dr. Khalil Suleiman headed up the Emergency Ambulance Team of the Red Crescent Society in Jenin. This medical doctor ran a maternity center in the area and taught part time at our university. He was killed at age sixty-one in Jenin Camp when the ambulance he was riding in was fired at by an Israeli tank. The Israeli army carried out raids in Jenin Camp in search of suspected Palestinian militants.

Jenin Camp is one of nineteen Palestinian refugee camps in the West Bank and another thirty-nine camps in Jordan, Lebanon, Syria, Gaza, and East Jerusalem. The camps were established by the United Nations Relief and Works Agency, UNRWA, to assist about 750,000 Palestinians who lost their homes and livelihood due to the war in 1948.[5]

According to UNRWA, today there are 5.6 million Palestinian refugees eligible for UNRWA services.[6] These include Palestinians displaced in 1948 and 1967 and their descendants.

Jenin Camp, less than a quarter of a square mile, is home to about 14,000 people, including 12,250 refugees.[7] The camp sits on the western edge of the city of Jenin.

I stood with Waleed on a make-shift stage in front of several hundred residents of the camp and our university delegation, all on their feet in the March sun. The international teachers and I wore black-and-white *keffiyeh* scarves around our necks. The *keffiyeh* is a symbol of Palestinian nationalism, and we meant to show solidarity with the Palestinian community. We were gathered outside the United Nations Girls' School, where camp leaders welcomed us.

Board member Ghaleb had had the idea for the Jenin Camp visit a few days before. Ghaleb, Waleed, and I sat in outdoor seating at the new Zaytouna Restaurant on the ground floor of our campus apartment building. Amidst the music, loud conversations, and cascading waterfall over Fred Flintstone-style rocks at the Zaytouna, we talked about Dr. Khalil's death and the devastation in the refugee camp.

Suddenly, Ghaleb proposed, "Let's go to Jenin Camp, a group from the university, to show our support for the people there." I saw his mind spinning as he thought about one more way to connect the university with the community. "Dr. Waleed can speak for the university, and Cynthia can speak for the international teachers."

My speech was in simple Arabic, since I had wanted to write my own speech and speak without translation: "We have come to share your sorrow and your pain. We know that you are suffering. May God help you and be with you."

I continued, "We have stayed here in this difficult situation because we want to help your children get their education, because education is your future and your hope. We understand the situation you are living in, and we feel with you. We want all people to understand your situation, so we write letters to people we know and to newspapers in our countries. We wish peace for you and for all Palestinian people. May God be with you."

After the speeches and words of thanks from camp leaders, our group of seventy walked through the streets of the camp. We passed crumbled walls and stairways of houses, charred buildings, bullet holes, and shattered glass. The burnt ambulance in which Dr. Khalil had been killed sat empty and silent. People shared stories of the Israeli occupation of the camp. An elderly man told me how he and his wife had cowered against the wall of their living room for hours. They had held a mattress to their bodies as a shield against bullets flying through their house. A young man showed me the wound in his abdomen, shot as he sat in his bedroom. A woman recounted the shelling in the streets. People described how the soldiers had taken over their houses and used them as outposts, forbidding family members from using the toilet or telephone. Each family we passed shared a sobering experience.

That day in March reminded me that almost every student I taught and colleague with whom I worked had his or her own story to share. Almost everyone knew someone who had been injured, killed, detained, or arrested. My students had seen the damage of property and the destruction of life. It's remarkable, I thought, that my students keep studying.

"You are Palestinian now. You are one of us," my students said to me after my words at Jenin Camp. That also felt remarkable. I wanted to stand in solidarity with the Palestinian people, especially with my students.

The following month in April 2002, I visited Jenin Refugee Camp again, this time after the Israeli army's much bigger invasion into the camp. With armored vehicles, tanks, and bulldozers, the

Israeli Defense Forces made incursions into six major Palestinian cities in Area A, including Jenin, what they called Operation Defensive Shield. They targeted Jenin Camp after a series of Palestinian suicide bombings and attacks against Israeli soldiers and civilians. The incursion in Jenin Camp lasted ten days and captured worldwide attention.

The United Nations reported that 52 Palestinians, both militants and civilians, and 23 Israeli soldiers were killed, though Israel blocked a first-hand investigation.[8] According to UNRWA, more than 400 homes were destroyed and more than 3,500 residents became homeless.[9] The Palestinians I spoke with gave much higher figures and called the event a massacre.

"You see what the Jewish did to our homes?" people said as Waleed, another teacher, and I passed by the huge pile of rubble where they had lived. Women were sitting on the ground, consoling one another. A man was digging among the wreckage, searching for the money he had buried under his house for safe keeping. Children were rooting through the debris, looking for pieces of metal or plastic to use as toys. As I looked at a twisted wheelchair, an older man came up to me. He told me about the young man who had been in the wheelchair, killed when the army demolished his family's house.

"*Haram,*" I kept repeating. This is against God's laws! "*Mish maoul,*" I added. I cannot believe it! After the visit, we went to Ghaleb's house, joining his wife and five children for lunch. But it was hard to eat.

University classes were cancelled for most of April with strict curfews imposed by the Israeli army. Jenin was cut off from the rest of the West Bank. When classes did resume, Jenin and Jenin Refugee Camp were on everybody's minds. Students in different levels of English classes wrote about their experiences:

In April the Israeli army invaded Jenin and Jenin Camp. More than 1000 soldiers, 100 tanks, and 6 Apache helicopters entered Jenin. The first day my mother and I woke up to the sound of tanks. What is that like? The electricity was cut, the water was cut, and the telephone was cut. In my opinion, the life stopped. In the house we had little food, a little water in the well. The soldiers announced, "No one can leave their homes. The markets are closed." My father in Saudi Arabia could not call because the telephone was cut. My father became worry. In the night we used candles to light the house. This continued for many days. The time passed very slowly. This was a complex and bad experience.

In many parts of this world, you can see the trace of destruction. The reason for this destruction is sometimes environmental, maybe earthquakes, volcanoes, or storms. The destruction in Jenin happened by the human hand of Israel. The army came to Jenin and removed all kinds of mercy from their hearts. They started to destroy the buildings and kill the people without caring. They didn't stop there, but they continued their mission by cutting the water and electricity to let the Palestinians live without water for 15 days. They didn't stop there, but they spread snipers everywhere to shoot anybody moving in the streets. The injured people didn't have ambulances because the army destroyed most of the ambulances and prevented doctors and nurses from helping the injured people, letting them bleed to death. If you go to Jenin Camp now,

you can see the destruction everywhere. You can smell death everywhere from burned and decaying bodies. You can hear the crying of children and the mothers who lost their relatives. How much time does the world need to stop these crimes?

On the first Friday in May 2002, a couple hundred students, faculty, and staff assembled in Jenin at 7:00 in the morning, wearing jeans and AAUP T-shirts. With brooms, buckets, dust pans, or pieces of cardboard to serve as dust pans, we scooped up piles of rubble from the streets into a big trash heap. We spread out over several blocks of bullet-sprayed buildings, smashed vehicles, torn-up blacktop, and debris. Shop owners greeted us and lent us supplies.

As I swept, I pondered what the Israeli army had done in two years' time. Whole sections of the city, including the police station and other government facilities, had been leveled. I wondered how Jenin could provide civil and security control when their government buildings had been bombed. Later, a friend would show me the bullet holes in the outside wall of her house. The city is ruined, I thought. I had never seen anything like it.

The next morning on Saturday, photographs of students sweeping the streets of Jenin decorated the university entrance hall. Waleed was in almost every photo. We all felt proud of him.

13

Carrying on through Chaos

"What should I do?" a teacher asked. "Only four students showed up in my 9:00 a.m. class." Another teacher said, "Students are saying there are no classes today. Is it true?" Yet another question was "Do you know what's going on?"

Not knowing myself what was happening, I needed to guide my teachers. "We haven't received any notice that classes are cancelled. I'm waiting to hear. Until then, I suggest you go to your classroom at the beginning of each class period, see how many students show up, and then decide what to do," I advised.

I tried to get updates from Waleed if he was not busy negotiating with students or discussing options with advisors. I peeked my head in his open door and did not need to say anything as he looked up from his desk. "We're still working on it," he would say or "We haven't made a decision yet. I will let you know."

The second academic year was extraordinary in terms of both achievements and difficulties. The curfews during and after the Jenin Camp invasion were not the only ones. Israeli closures and killings began in September 2001 and stretched throughout the year. Sometimes, this followed a Palestinian attack. Or the Israeli army would claim to be looking for people on their wanted list. Whatever the reason, when the Israeli army or checkpoints appeared, it was difficult for students to get to campus. While about

20% of students lived on campus in the women's dorm, about 50% of the student body, mainly young men, rented apartments in nearby Zababdeh. Around 30% of students were commuters, who came from either Jenin, villages close by, or towns and cities further away.

When students were absent because of Israeli curfews, closures, checkpoints, or arrests, the university administration expected faculty to respond accordingly. That meant offering students the chance to make up what they had missed. My Palestinian colleagues modeled unending patience, meeting with students in their offices.

The administration sent memos to guide us in our work. During the December exam period, Jenin was closed after suicide bombings in Jerusalem and Haifa. Waleed informed faculty that classes would continue no matter how many students attended. He asked faculty to (1) give no exams, (2) offer only review sessions and discussion periods during class hours, and (3) report the number of students attending each class to Academic Affairs for an ongoing analysis of the situation. For the remaining three class days, only 70%, 60%, and then 58% of my students attended.

My job as a teacher was a delicate one. I needed to keep sight of course objectives, maintain standards, and treat all students fairly while being mindful of the circumstances. As a director, I needed to encourage my teachers to do the same. Every day was a learning experience for us since no precedents existed for the complexities of this life.

"Please try to work with students who are absent because of a curfew," I told my teachers. "They should not be at a disadvantage. But you do not need to pass them just because they face difficulties. Students should pass based on their language proficiency and readiness to move to the next level."

Not only were students absent a lot, but classes were frequently cancelled. The killing of a key Palestinian political figure by the Israeli army or a bombing raid in Gaza meant the possibility of cancelled classes and the certainty of chaos and disorder.

"In the Arab world, you are not supposed to behave normally during the three days of mourning after a death," Samah explained to me. "For some students, going to class is like betraying the Palestinian cause." I could count on Samah to explain things.

According to the university policy, all cancelled classes were to be announced officially in writing by the Office of the President or Academic Affairs. Students, however, often took matters into their own hands. A mob of ten or twenty students would stomp through the halls with a megaphone, shouting in Arabic, "There are no classes today! Classes are cancelled!"

Once, I walked up to the student leader of a march through the halls. I knew the student and asked him to put down his megaphone. "Your voice is loud enough," I pleaded. "You don't need it." Without the megaphone, the students continued their march.

In Waleed's office, I protested, "You told me that the student leaders agreed not to use megaphones inside the buildings." I felt my face flush.

Visibly upset with me, Waleed asserted, "Cynthia, you need to be careful. You could get hurt."

"The students are not going to hurt me," I said, my mouth getting dry. "We just want to teach our classes without interruptions."

"You don't realize what they can do. We have to avoid violence at all costs," Waleed insisted.

I did not fully comprehend the harm that students could bring to the university or the risks involved in going against their demands. Waleed explained that students could chain doors shut, prevent cars from moving, and even burn buildings.

Waleed spent much of his time with student leaders, discussing how to respond after an attack by the Israeli army. When a general strike was dictated by the governing Palestinian Authority or the Palestinian Ministry of Higher Education, no classes were held. Otherwise, Waleed and the students needed to reach an agreement. The end was usually a compromise, like canceling one or two class periods so students could hold a demonstration, instead of canceling a whole day as the students wanted.

Waleed's last name, Deeb, means "wolf," and I thought it suited him well. Intelligent, strong, and guarding the pack, Waleed knew how to work with students. Yet sometimes, the students were restless. Even if they had agreed to a compromise with Waleed, they did not think students should be in class after an Israeli offense.

My students and I were settled into a lesson one day when I heard commotion in the hall outside. Suddenly, the door burst open, and five or six male students tromped in. Their necks were wrapped in black-and-white *keffiyehs,* which symbolized affiliation with the Fatah political party, the dominant Palestinian party at that time led by Yasser Arafat. One of the taller students shouted in Arabic, "You should get out of the classroom now! How can you sit and study when your brothers have been killed?"

I turned to the intruders and asked them to leave, reminding them of the policy against entering classes in session. Then I turned to my students and offered, "If you want to leave, you may. I will continue class with those who stay, but whatever you decide is fine." Everyone stayed in their seats.

Students had mixed reactions to having class on those chaotic days. When only a handful of students turned up, we put our chairs in a circle and discussed what was going on. I asked the students, "What do you think the university should do? Do you think we should have class?"

"We want to study, but it is difficult," they answered. "If we stay in the classroom when the other students tell us to go out, it is not good. They will think we are not with the Palestinians. We have to show our support for our people."

If too many classes were cancelled, we had to make them up. Extending the semester was one option, while holding class six days a week was another. In December, I informed my teachers that they were expected to teach on Thursdays, our weekend, and that their midyear break had been cut short by two weeks.

Teachers were already overloaded with large classes and more teaching hours than their contracts required due to a persistent shortage of teachers. Asking them to work on Thursdays was pushing the limits, I thought.

In the spring, we were again teaching six days a week for a period of six weeks, making up for lost time after the Jenin Camp invasion. Palestinian teachers across disciplines grumbled to Waleed during a university-wide faculty meeting. "The students are tired. We are tired."

We were not just physically worn but emotionally exhausted as well. One of my teachers told me in a separate meeting, "My good will is at zero."

I tried to satisfy both my teachers who were disgruntled and those who did not share their sentiments. I received several notes, including the following: *Dear Cynthia, I just wanted to let you know that I'm sorry if I've appeared ungrateful for your efforts. I appreciate your acting as my point of contact with the administration. I've had some time to think about the Thursday teaching and concluded that it's really no big deal. I'll do my best to not add to your worries.*

What we had to do, I believed, was to try to stay positive, to make every effort, and to do the best that we could do. "I'm doing my best" became another mantra of mine.

Like all teachers, we were listeners, counselors, and advocates. When a student told me, "I have a headache, I did not sleep well," he or she was probably not exaggerating. While I *heard* about atrocities, my students *experienced* them. A bad night for me meant there were mosquitoes, or there was no hot water. A bad night for my students meant something else: being forced outside in the street by Israeli soldiers while their homes were searched and furniture was destroyed, trying to fall asleep to the sound of tanks in the streets or helicopters overhead, having a neighbor, relative or friend arrested, injured or killed. This went on during all my years in Palestine. My students talked about and wrote their stories:

> *One evening the Israeli army occupied our home. About 20 soldiers entered the building. They broke all the windows and spoiled my grandfather's house. The soldiers put my grandfather in the sitting room alone. They wouldn't allow him to go out. They stayed there for 8 hours. Next the soldiers went to my uncle's house in the same building. My parents and I didn't move from our house. The soldiers left the building with my uncle and put him in a tank. They arrested him. His children were beginning to cry. They thought that the army wanted to kill their father. When the soldiers left, we could move to my grandfather's and uncle's homes and see what the soldiers did. It was in a very bad condition. The rooms were untidy. The chairs, tables, and beds were broken. The clothes were one over another. My grandfather found that his money had been*

stolen. My uncle returned after one month. He was very thin. I asked my God to live in peace, and I prayed a lot. This is my story, but it is simple if we compare it with other stories.

To acknowledge my students' reality of oppression, I asked them at the beginning of each day, "What happened last night? How are the roads today? Did you face checkpoints this morning?"

Our curriculum file called *The Situation* thickened. Vocabulary words relevant to *Al-Wade'* were divided into lists of nouns and verbs in specific categories. Nouns of destruction included *air strike, bulldozer, demolition, incursion, invasion, siege,* and *tank*. Verbs of treatment included *force, hit, humiliate, push, punch, slap,* and *threaten*.

A handout entitled *Language of the Oppressor and Oppressed* listed the distinct terms used by Israelis and Palestinians to refer to the same thing. What Israelis call *terrorist,* Palestinians call *freedom fighter*. What Israelis call *terrorist organization,* Palestinians call *resistance movement*. *Suicide bombing* versus *operation*. *Suicide bomber* versus *martyr*. *Targeted killing* versus *assassination*. *Jenin security operation* versus *Jenin massacre*.

A fill-in-the-blanks worksheet focused on being stopped by soldiers at a checkpoint. A news article described a suicide bombing and the Israeli army's destruction of the bomber's home in response.

An article from my hometown newspaper gave students the chance to read my views about their country—the land, people, and culture—which I had reported to someone else.

At the same time, sensitivity to all students in a class was important. A female student said to me when I was visiting classes and observing teachers, "I don't want to talk about The Situation all the time." Not wanting to neglect other issues, during the first week of every semester, I asked my students to list three topics that they would like to discuss. From their suggestions, I was reminded that even students in Palestine living under military occupation are interested in sports, culture, technology, friendship, and love.

Students at the university fell in love just like students around the world. One day a likable, rather quiet student named Ali, whose belt was pulled tight around his thin waist, appeared in my office, grinning as usual. "Teacher, can I have a copy of a photograph on your door?" The photograph Ali wanted was a snapshot of his classmates taken at the end of a semester, women in the front row, men in the back. Ali told me shyly, "I need this picture because I love a girl in the picture." I walked over to my door with Ali and asked him to show me which girl. He pointed her out and said, "Please, Teacher, I really need this picture."

"If she comes and tells me it's okay with her, then I will give you the picture," I told him.

Life felt normal after all, as I thought about people falling in love. I was in love myself, with Bob miles away in Mexico.

Before emergence of the term "the new normal," I thought about my life and life in Palestine in terms of normality. As The Situation continued to escalate, life seemed absurd at times. Nothing was normal anymore. The abnormal became normal. I thought, If I can see each day with all its abnormalities as somehow normal, then I can continue living in this situation. But until Palestinians have the normal life they deserve, I will not be satisfied.

14

Recruiting

It was ironic that during the Israeli invasion of Jenin Refugee Camp, I was in the U.S. on a recruiting trip. The Situation had been heating up so much that I was unable to print our recruiting brochures before I left. The print shops were too busy printing martyr posters—posters of Palestinians who were killed at the hands of the Israeli army or those who died while fighting the Palestinian fight for freedom. Because of the demand for martyr posters, I had to print the brochures in the States.

Our advertisement for recruiting stated proudly the first year, *The university opened in October 2000 and has remained open in spite of the ongoing crisis in the region.*

The second year we added more: *In spite of the ongoing crisis in the region, teachers here enjoy the stimulation of being involved in a relatively new university, experience the peacefulness of the hills around campus, and gain an insider's perspective on the Palestinian-Israeli conflict.*

Two years later, there would be another addition: *Due to the occupation, teachers need to be flexible and adaptable in both working and living environments.*

While I was at the convention of Teachers of English to Speakers of Other Languages, TESOL, in Salt Lake City, Utah, other recruiters were surprised to see a booth at the employment clearinghouse representing the Arab American University in Jenin. Having heard of Jenin in the news, they seemed impressed that a university there would still be open. Several stopped by to chat. When I thought about it, it was mind-boggling that the university had stayed open through all the ups and downs.

AAUP sought to hire highly proficient speakers of English for the language center to help build the solid English-language environment that the administration and founders desired. A master's degree and teaching experience were required.

Finding and keeping international faculty was not easy. In my five years at AAUP, I saw over thirty teachers from abroad come and go. They left their homes in North America, the United Kingdom, Australia, Norway, Switzerland, and Germany. They were American, Canadian, British, Scottish, Pakistani, Australian, Norwegian, Danish, Italian, and Iranian. They came because they valued cross-cultural experience, believed in global exchange, and loved language, teaching, travel, and adventure.

Most stayed only one year. A handful left before the end of their contracts. Several needed to be let go.

One teacher left only several weeks after arriving, and I could not say I was sorry. Minutes before a placement test in September the first year, I discovered that the pencils we had purchased were not sharpened. We were expecting about 300 students, and the university did not have electric pencil sharpeners. Knowing I could not sharpen all the pencils in time by myself, I gave each of the three teachers a couple boxes of pencils and a manual sharpener and asked for their help. The teacher, a well-dressed woman slightly older than I, shouted at me in a cocky voice that reverberated down the hall, "I did not get a master's degree to sharpen pencils! If we start doing this now, they'll always expect it of us!" At first, I thought she was joking but soon realized she was not when she added, "I will not carry books or chairs to the test room either, so don't ask me!"

With the high turnover rate and an ongoing shortage of teachers for the classes we needed to offer, we were constantly recruiting. The lack of teachers did not mean a lack of interest. Over a five-year period, we received hundreds of responses to our online advertisements, and we interviewed 125 candidates, mainly by telephone. While some applied out of no particular interest in Palestine, others were passionate and informed. Many were highly qualified with excellent teaching experience.

They asked pertinent questions—about the apartment furniture, dust and mold, electricity and hot water, foods available, food costs, telephone services, internet access, the weather, the weekends, exercise facilities, pianos, visas, medical facilities, SARS, dress restrictions, experience of women, program matters, whether students had the freedom to express themselves, extracurricular activities, what I found challenging, what I enjoyed.

Two applicants were Jewish. But Waleed thought it would be unwise to hire a Jew to work at a West Bank university at such an intense time. "It's too risky," he asserted. "I don't think our students are ready for that."

We needed teachers who were both competent in the classroom and capable of coping with The Situation. I did not want anyone to arrive unaware, so my letter to applicants was candid. I described what it was like to live in isolation in a volatile political situation with restricted mobility, uncertain status, frequent visa runs, and harassment from soldiers. I clarified that not everything at AAUP ran smoothly, paychecks were often late, students were just beginning to develop their language skills, and student motivation and study habits were impacted by the occupation.

For those and other reasons, most candidates turned down our job offers.

My moods coincided with the ups and downs of recruiting. It was like being on a roller-coaster ride—one night elated when a candidate accepted, the next night glum when an applicant declined. Bob got to hear all about it and share my emotions when we talked.

Listening to candidates speak of their experiences took my mind back to my own happy moments in the classroom over many years. Recruiting reminded me of the wonder of teaching.

English Language Center team 2001-2002

English Language Center team 2004-2005

ELC team members: Lamees, Samah, Cynthia, and Kawther

Cynthia at her desk

Waleed's office—Jim on the left, Waleed second to the right

A section of the city of Jenin and surrounding area

AAUP students and staff sweeping Jenin streets, 2002

President Waleed Deeb in Jenin Refugee Camp, 2002

Jenin Camp rubble, including wheelchair

Children inside Jenin Camp

Roadblocks and a pop-up checkpoint

The Happy Van (top) and off-road driving

YEAR THREE

A question that crushes, shatters, perplexes, disturbs, shocks, bothers, annoys, and kills me is "when?" I have asked myself this question a thousand times. Every day, every night, and every morning I ask myself this question, but futilely. The answer is not within my capabilities. Until when shall we keep suffering as humans? Until when will we find ourselves dehumanized? To help myself find an answer, I read many books, novels, stories, literature, religious books, and philosophies of different people and cultures. Despite this, I'm still looking for the correct answer.

—Student, Arab American University of Palestine

15

Bob is Back

Meeting Bob in Palestine seemed to be my destiny. At the Nablus hotel where the university put us up for a few weeks during the first year, our rooms were side by side. When we moved to campus, our apartments were again next to each other.

Wherever Bob lived, he was painting. In his Nablus hotel room, he brushed splashes of orange, green, and yellow onto a canvas spread on the floor. In his apartment, I sat mesmerized as he worked on a canvas taped to his living room wall from floor to ceiling.

Wherever Bob lived, there was music. He strummed on his guitar and on the oud he had bought in Jenin. Flute and violin melodies wafted through the walls. Bob took his music to the stairway landing or the fourth-floor laundry room, the cement walls of our building carrying the sound well. Several of us joined him at times for acapella harmonizing in the echoing halls. It was hard to stay away when we heard him out there.

Bob liked to laugh. He had a fresh perspective and made everything fun. Giggle fits seemed to follow us around. As my mother later put it, "He adds color to our family." I, being more serious, noticed our differences right away. Bob—gentle and laid back. Me—assertive and easily unsettled. Bob—non-judgmental. Me—always looking for perfection, Miss Quality Control, as Bob calls me. I need structure and planning, whereas Bob likes to go with the flow. I am task-oriented and busy, while Bob takes time to see the world around him, nothing passing him by. Despite our differences, or because of them, we got together. We shared many things in common, like simplicity, the spiritual, a sense of adventure, interest in cultures, affection for relics, a love of nature, art, and music.

Separated during my second year in Palestine, we married later that summer in a small ceremony in Virginia. My friends and family welcomed Bob in, and his family welcomed me. My brother sent a talking clock with a photo of his family on one side. His children were young, ages six and four. Prepped by their dad, they cheered us: "Hi, Aunt Cynthia and Uncle Bob. This is Alyse and Austin. We just want to tell you that we love you. Goodbye." I would later use the clock for listening practice with my students.

Back in Palestine in the fall of 2002, my third year, Bob and I settled into a routine. I was busy in the English Language Center, and Bob was getting ready for his art classes. He was the first to teach drawing and painting electives at AAUP. Designing drawing benches, working with the carpenters who built them, and purchasing art supplies for each student were tasks to attend to. Free to develop class ideas, he wanted to make art fun.

A Palestinian artist named Mervat joined him. Bob and Mervat shared the same goal—to bring out students' creative potential through art. Mervat wore colorful tunics over her pants and matching scarves to cover her hair. Her colors and the antiques displayed in her office showed her artistic sense. Mervat was a single woman around our age. She not only befriended both of us but also introduced us to her friends.

Bob found a studio space in Zababdeh where he could do his own artistic work. Marrying in our forties, we were both used to independent living. We discovered both before and after we wed that we each needed alone time and space to do our own thing. Bob's studio gave him the space he needed.

Along the winding Zababdeh street, a metal gate opened into an airy courtyard, with 200-year-old layers of life built up around the rooms on each side. Bob's studio was off to the left. With thick stone walls covered over by plaster, tiny windows on two sides, and a nine-foot, arched ceiling, the studio was spacious and inviting, both to Bob and to visitors like me who stopped in. As Bob worked, people speaking Arabic walked by on the narrow street that wound into the center of town, and the Islamic call to prayer rang out over the loudspeaker. The work he created in that inspirational spot would later be shared with the community.

Back at home, I was happy to return from work and find Bob in Betty Crocker mode. Four-by-six photos of both our families trimmed the cupboards above the sink. A rice cooker, toaster, and electric kettle sat on the two-foot counter; a microwave sat on top of the fridge. In that space, Bob made what he called experiments: apple turnovers and cream puffs, tomato soup and salsa.

In Palestinian culture, the flat roof of one's home is like a room of the house, used for hanging laundry, holding water tanks, having barbeques, and enjoying evening breezes. The roof of our apartment building was no different, with a stunning 360-degree view. In our first year of marriage, we sometimes lay side by side atop a soft blanket on the hard concrete of the roof, gazing up at the stars. I knew the big and little dippers, and Bob pointed out many other constellations.

Below us in our apartment building, the Zaytouna Restaurant buzzed with loud chatter. Inside the restaurant, standard fare was served: *falafel, hummus, baba ghanouj, kufta,* fries, and *shish taouk.* In the outside section, laughter flowed freely, along with cigarette smoke. But what set the real ambience were the water pipes, known as *nargila* in Palestinian Arabic. The smell of apple or mint tobacco was classic Zaytouna.

At 9:00 p.m. the restaurant closed, and cars drove into the distance. The tick of our clock and the hum of our fridge drew us into a lull. "It's so quiet," we said to each other, sitting on the sofa. In winter, the rain would drum down on the roof above us. During wheat harvest, the thrasher would run all night. Roosters from our neighboring village, Talfit, could crow anytime. And anytime, Israel could show up with its military might. But mostly, it was quiet.

It was only quiet, however, until the wild dogs commenced their cries. Their barking began around midnight when we were already asleep. The longing howls in the hills sometimes woke us up and kept us awake until they faded in the distance. The dogs' next dirge was around 5:00 a.m., when we usually got up anyway.

"Did you dream?" Bob asked upon waking. We sometimes lay in bed and shared our night dreams, having both paid attention to dreams for years before we met.

Bob backed me up emotionally. After a hard day at work, I walked into our apartment and was greeted by Bob, asking, "What can I get you, *Habibti*," an Arabic term of endearment. "You just sit down and put your feet up while I make dinner." I plopped on the sofa and looked at the painting on the wall. Bob had transformed the colorful splashes from the Nablus hotel room into images of olives, stairways, flying carpets, and angels, a painting we called "Magic Carpet." As I gazed at Bob's imaginary landscape, I felt grateful for the magic that had brought us together and for Bob, who pampered me. He seemed to know intuitively which days to call me in my office with his familiar, "What would you like for dinner?" He just as instinctively knew when to make rice, my comfort food.

He encouraged me to work less, to put in a ten-hour day, not more. But he never pushed me when I did not follow his advice. Except one night, he had had enough. I worked until 11:30 p.m. that night, having gone to the office at 6:00 a.m. When I got home, my whole body, especially my back, felt broken.

"Can I get a massage, *Habibi*?" I asked, a common request of mine.

For the first time ever, Bob refused: "I told you I wasn't giving massages after 9:00 p.m." As I tried to get to sleep that night, I thought about his message and knew that he was right—I needed to change my habits.

Bob's listening ear helped me keep going when I thought about giving up. I am amazed when I think about how often I came home needing to talk about the same old frustrations at work, and rarely did he say, "You already told me that yesterday." I realize now more than I did then how much I came to depend on him. Bob's simple art of listening gave me new energy.

16

English at AAUP

The best in the region. That is what a brochure I was editing for Public Relations stated. Really? I cringed. We were just a new university, and not everything was that good. I am not competitive by nature, and assertions like that had always bothered me. I did not think just one of anything needed to stand out or be awarded.

Though I did not buy into the university's claim to being the best in the region, the mandate to foster a strong English program motivated me to do *my* best. The enthusiasm of the English Language Center team energized me. Class evaluations encouraged me. Most students were pleased with their progress. As their language skills improved, their confidence grew.

I had visited several high schools in the area and felt confident myself that our program offered an effective follow-up to the more traditional, grammar-based approach to language learning that focused on exams and grades.

I believed learning English would not only expand students' career opportunities but also enrich their lives. In my own experience, learning language had gone hand in hand with learning about cultures and developing relationships. Since high school, when migrant workers from Mexico and refugees from Vietnam came to Archbold, Ohio, my hometown, I had enjoyed getting to know people from other places. Comments on student evaluations pointed to a similar kind of broadening:

The course improve our character and strengthen the relationship between students.

* * *

It increase the knowledge in everything, not just in English, and help us to know more about life.

* * *

It is interesting to learn with American teacher and to see how the American people is lovely.

* * *

The teacher, she was like a friend, like a mother, and like a sister.

The English Language Center was abuzz with activity as each new semester rolled around. By the fall of our third year in 2002, AAUP had over 2,000 students, and our center worked with 800 of them. Eight internationals and seven Palestinians made up our team.

A new Palestinian teacher just out of college came bouncing up to me after her very first class. "Oh, I love teaching!" she proclaimed. That is the kind of person we were lucky enough to find.

Samah was savvy with her work, but she was more than just an assistant. Her outbursts—"Wow, wow, wow!" or "Hey, hey,

hey!"— buoyed up our days. She came in close when she spoke, talked with her hands, always smiling. Though fun-loving, her "How are you?" was sincere. Sometimes, she and I closed my office door, sat in my cushioned wicker chairs, and passed the tissues as we shared deeply about our lives.

Others on our team were equally passionate, caring, and animated. Almost everyone loved to talk. Some loved to eat but never gained weight. Others loved to eat and then announce, "I'm on a new diet. It's great!" A few loved to smoke. When we went on group hikes, some puffed on their cigarettes all the way up the mountain.

The bulk of the team ranged in age from twenty to thirty, with a handful of us a bit older. "*Yalla*! Come to Cynthia's office! We're having a party!" My office became a gathering place for both planned and spontaneous affairs.

In weekly meetings, the fifteen of us sat around the conference table in my office. The carpenters on campus had crafted the large table from laminate. Around that oval table with a plant in the middle, we listened and learned from each other. "What our students need.... I was thinking.... What if we tried...?" Even when strong opinions were expressed, the laughter was contagious.

The college deans, whose council meetings I attended, agreed that a block of time during the week set aside for student activities would be beneficial. Because of The Situation and the need for commuting students to get home before dark, after-school activities were rare. The Deans Council approved Saturday, Monday, and Wednesday from 1:00 to 2:00 p.m. as the Student Activities period. In our newly established Media Center, students could read English language magazines, like *National Geographic, Good Housekeeping, Newsweek,* and *PC World.*

Movies and Conversation Hours continued. Conversation Hour became so popular in the third year that it was difficult to find enough rooms for the 200 interested students. In small groups, students discussed issues like The Situation, cultural differences, and women's rights.

Our efforts invigorated our whole team. Though we met hurdles, and our students' skills did not magically improve overnight, we did see steady progress over time. I knew that was how language learning worked anyway.

I had learned in a previous job that expecting too much could be counterproductive when a colleague had said to me, "Your perfectionism can be intimidating." Doing our best is what I now expected of both my teachers and myself. When frustrated by what we could not achieve, I reminded myself of my mantra, "We're doing the best that we can."

17

Loud Voices

A dozen children marched in the dusty, side street of the small town of Zababdeh, pretending to be demonstrators. Boys as young as two followed the seven- and eight-year-old leaders, stomping and shouting slogans at the top of their little lungs. On an errand in town, I was taken aback.

On different occasions on the university campus, white plastic chairs were arranged in rows, and a stage with a podium and microphone was set up. The overflow crowd stood in the back. Attendees squinted under the sun's glare. Flags flew, and students donned scarves with political party affiliation patterns in red, green, black, and white.

I sometimes showed up at student-led demonstrations, wanting to listen and support. Whether a student translated for me, or I relied on myself, the message rang loud and clear:

> Death to Israel. Death to Zionism. The army of Muhammad will defeat the Zionist army. We sacrifice our life for Palestine. Death is better than surrendering. Jerusalem is our capital. Jerusalem is in our heart. Millions will march to Al-Aqsa Mosque to liberate Al-Aqsa.

The one- and two-hour demonstrations wore me down. The rhetoric dismayed me even if it was familiar, even if it was important to my students. Am I in the right place? I asked myself. Should I stay here in Palestine with all these loud voices? Silent protests and candlelight vigils had been more my style.

People always seemed to be shouting. TV news showed angry mobs crying out in the streets. Speakers at rallies tried to outshout one another. Protestors in crowds lost their voices after straining them. Even at nonpolitical events, like the inauguration of a language lab I attended at a nearby high school, bellowing out political messages was the norm.

At the inauguration, a petite middle-aged woman read a nine-page Arabic poem she had written filled with rhetoric about Jerusalem and Palestine. I counted the pages as she flipped each one over. The projection of her voice in the microphone was piercing:

> This school will help people build their homeland. This place will help people fight the occupation. This place will help people drive Israel out. I hope for the day when I will live in a free Palestine with Jerusalem as its capital.

Waleed, who had attended the inauguration, later gave me his perspective on the shouting: "When you recite a poem in Arabic, you say it in a loud voice. You want to show that you are emotional. You want your audience to feel how intense it is. You cannot talk about liberating Palestine in a soft voice. If you lose your voice, it means you gave it your best."

I asked Waleed about children in schools that I had witnessed shouting out their answers in English class. He clarified, "If you speak in a soft voice, that means you are shy, and that is not good. Shouting the answer is good; it shows your strong personality." No wonder Bob wore ear plugs when he taught noisy pupils at the Arab American School, I thought.

By the time Bob returned to Palestine, the elementary school had moved to a location in the city of Jenin. Attending a school celebration there, I saw again how not only loud voices but also The Situation permeated all of life. The fourth-grade students performed a play about a village wedding. At the end of the wedding reception in the play, Israeli soldiers came in and shot the ten-year-old groom dead, and the play ended as a Shakespearean tragedy. The girls wailed, and the boys lifted the martyr above their heads, parading his body around, yelling.

How tragic, I thought. This play mirrors real life, even for fourth graders.

18

Palestinian Hospitality

My Palestinian students made sweeping statements: "Americans are not close to their families." Is that so? I thought. I felt close to my family.

My students announced, "Americans don't like to cook. They eat hamburgers and fast food." Really? I pondered. I wondered if I should show my students my recipe book or tell them what I had cooked the week before.

Sometimes, I made a declaration to try to break down student stereotypes: "My husband has eight brothers."

"Is that true?" came the surprised response. "He is not like Americans. He is like Palestinians."

On an English placement test, students wrote about whether they wanted to have a large or small family. While some saw the benefits of two or three children, many wanted families like Bob's. In writing, students gave a glimpse of their homes. Families of eight, nine, or ten were not uncommon. When writing about their best friend, many students chose their mothers.

"I want you to meet my family. I want to show you my village. When can you come?" my students entreated. An invitation to a student's home was a family affair. We chatted with not only our students but also their parents and grandparents, brothers and sisters, cousins, aunts, and uncles. Everyone was welcome. I could see why students planned to live in their hometowns and villages after graduating.

Four male students walked me through the hilly streets of their village, Anza, one Friday after midday prayers. They pointed out their school, their houses, and the olive press. We were all invited to one of the students' homes for lunch. In Maher's home, smells of *musakhan,* a Palestinian delicacy, filled the house. Homemade flat bread, round and big like an extra-large pizza, is covered with onions, pieces of chicken, and the deep red spice sumac and is then baked in the oven. The flavors blend and soak the bread with tasty, oily juice. *Musakhan* is reserved for special events or guests. The four young men and I sat at the table and talked with Maher's father, while Maher's mother made sure we were eating. "I am very proud of my son," Maher's father said. "I am very happy we have a university in Jenin." Maher seemed pleased to have his English teacher in his home.

Friday was visiting day in Palestine. One Friday, Bob and I were invited to Mr. Qadeem's house in a neighboring village, Im Tut. We had first met Qadeem a few weeks earlier in Jenin while searching for honey, a hard-to-get product in Palestine. Walking by his small Jenin food store, we spotted a large honeycomb sitting in a baking pan on the counter, alongside several jars of honey. Though we had just met, Qadeem arranged a date for us to come to his home.

After a warm welcome, Qadeem and his family, including Naira, a female student at AAUP, gave us a tour of their property. They raised rabbits, doves, chickens, goats, and honeybees. They made their daily bread over an open fire on a thin metal disk. A year's supply of olives, olive oil, and grape leaves filled up their storage room. How do you get the flat, dark grape leaves into the small-necked soda bottles? I wondered.

Inside the house, Qadeem's children served us juice and a slab of honeycomb on a plate. "*Masha* Allah—Wow!" we exclaimed when we saw the size of the chunk.

Qadeem said, "*Itfaddalu*, please eat," and we delved in. While we enjoyed this sweet appetizer, Qadeem told us a story.

One day on his way to Jenin with a truckload of supplies for his store, Qadeem was stopped at a pop-up checkpoint which had appeared suddenly. The young Israeli soldiers, guns in view, forced him to empty his truck and place everything on the ground. While reloading his truck with the sun beating down, Qadeem asked himself, how can these young soldiers, not much older than my own son, tell a middle-aged man like me what to do? Determined not to face such humiliation again, he made the decision to become self-sufficient at home, raising animals for food, rather than rely on his Jenin grocery store for income.

Though life outside on the roads was unfair, inside Palestinian homes, the atmosphere was lively. We joined Qadeem's family around the kitchen table for a lunch of warm bread, white cheese, honey, and fig jam, all homemade. This was my preferred kind of meal—where we each dipped our bread into common dishes spread out in the table's center.

With coffee and fruit in the living room afterwards, Qadeem said, "I'm glad my daughter can attend the Arab American University. I want her to have a good education and a successful career in the future. I want the same for her brother who will join the university in another year."

We strolled outside before leaving. It was a custom in Palestine to take a walk, gather on the flat roof, or sit under the shade of a tree in the late afternoon. Olive and almond trees rustled in the wind, and the family pointed out the homes of their relatives nearby. It was also a custom for families to live close to each other. Brothers shared land with brothers, and parents lived with the eldest son.

In other homes, Bob and I shared fast-breaking meals with friends during Ramadan. In the month of Ramadan, when practicing Muslims do not eat or drink from dawn to dusk, every day is visiting day. Food preparation gets special attention during this month of fasting, and every fast-breaking meal, called *iftar*, becomes a feast. *Iftar* is eaten after the sun goes down, first a dried date, then a sip of water, then a light soup. A full spread of meats, vegetables, rice or pasta, and salad follows, all placed on a cloth on the living room floor with everyone sitting on the floor on cushions. Dessert and coffee round out the meal, along with hearty conversation.

Ibrahim was the young man eager to speak English with me my first weeks at AAUP. He invited another American teacher couple and Bob and me to his village home in Al-Judeida for *iftar*. After the meal, I had the pleasure of dressing up in traditional Palestinian wear. Ibrahim's three little daughters with curly hair played in the courtyard outside the house. On a far side of the living room where we had eaten, Bob and the men sat chatting on pink-flowered floor mats. Framed diplomas and large framed photographs of family members who had died adorned the walls. A strand of artificial flowers was draped along the top of one wall.

At the other end of the room, Ibrahim's wife, mother, and sister-in-law brought out their collection of colored gowns for Samantha and me to see. Each region of Palestine claimed a unique design for their hand-embroidered, floor-length dresses made of cotton or velvet.

"Would you like to try one on?" the women asked Samantha and me in Arabic.

We looked at each other and nodded our heads, "Yes, of course," we answered in Arabic.

Donning the gowns, we eyed ourselves in the mirror and took photos with the women, smiling all the while. *"Shukran,"* we said, thanking the women for these memorable moments. *"Shukran,"* we all thanked Ibrahim for welcoming us to his home.

Another person who opened her home and heart was Amal, the woman who cleaned the language center. I saw her each morning when she came into my office. Her long dress met the floor that she washed. Along with her mop and dust cloth, she always carried a warm smile. We often took a minute to chat, sharing mostly about our families.

With six children of her own, Amal wondered how many Bob and I wanted to have. She said to me one day after I had gotten married, "Forty-one years old is not too old to start a family."

"But Bob and I have twenty-six nieces and nephews, friends with children we love, and students. Our students are like children to us," I explained.

Amal changed her thinking in time. She came to understand our view. Once, when she was cleaning my office, she heard another Palestinian woman ask me, "When do you and Mr. Bob plan to have children?"

Instead of me, Amal answered, "Their students are their children."

Amal had left school at a young age to help her mother at home with cleaning, cooking, and caring for siblings. Because she never learned to read or write, Amal wanted her own children to get a good education, maybe to attend university.

Amal did not know how to help her children with their schoolwork since she could not understand their textbooks. Whenever I visited her at home, I said to her two youngest daughters, Fatima and Haya, "Let me see your English workbooks." They each read aloud from their recent lessons, and we reviewed them together. I wasn't sure Fatima and Haya would master the English language, but the attention I gave the girls pleased Amal.

Amal worked six days a week at the university. On Fridays, her one day off, she did the laundry by hand, cleaned their two-room house, and cooked something special for her children. "I want to make something they love each week, even though I'm tired," she told me one Friday when I dropped by. She was preparing *wara aineb,* or stuffed grape leaves, one of my favorite foods. I sat down on the floor with her, reached for an empty grape leaf, then filled and rolled the leaves with her. With Amal, I felt at home.

Throughout my years in Palestine, one thing remained constant—the hospitality of the Palestinian people. No matter what people's outward circumstances, their homes were a place of warmth and family time, and I was welcomed to be a part.

19

Empowering Students

"What's the best method of resistance for Palestinians to achieve positive peace?" English teacher Jonathan asked his students in a class named Peace and Conflict. Jonathan had a stylish brown hairdo and a youthful look; he was not much older than our students. When he spoke, he held their attention.

The Peace and Conflict class was initiated by Suzanne, whose passion was Peace EFL, combining English as a Foreign Language teaching with conflict resolution. Suzanne, around my age, had trendy glasses and long, dark layered hair. She handed out hugs and kind words to her friends, we who knew her as Susie. Her sweet voice drew her students in.

Waleed, always open to new ideas and wanting to promote nonviolence among students, approved the new course in the university's third year.

In this advanced-level language course, students developed their reading, writing, listening, and speaking skills in English by studying the specific content of conflict and peace. The goal of the class was to give students language and a framework for analyzing and talking about their experiences of living in conflict. Students first looked at causes and theories of conflict. They then turned to what brings about peace.

In a debate I was invited to, students argued one of four positions: (1) violence, (2) strategic violence, (3) strategic nonviolence, or (4) nonviolence. Students had learned about opening statements, closing statements, and discussions of their position. Their debate impressed me. They expressed their opinions well, answered questions posed to them, and asked questions of the other side.

The paragraphs they wrote were equally impressive, not because they all chose nonviolence as I would have, but because they were learning to support their ideas with facts, statistics, and examples. When AAUP students first started college, they tended to make and repeat general statements like "The Jewish destroy our life" or "The Jewish don't want peace." We wanted to help them think critically on a new level.

> One student wrote, *Strategic violence in my opinion is the best method of resistance for Palestinian people. Strategic violence is more successful to remove the occupation because violence is the only language that Israelis understand. First, President Jamal Abdel Nasser said that anything taken by power can't be returned without power. When Israeli army took the Sinai from Egyptians by power, the Egyptian army got it back by power. The equation is very clear: power equals power. Second, I am sorry to say that the first intifada did not give the Palestinian people nothing; in fact, more settlements were built during the "peaceful years" than the years before, and nonviolence gave the Israelis a chance to take more land from us. Let me add that Palestinian people hate strategic violence, but the Jewish government imposed this method on the Palestinians. In this case, what can Palestinians do? The answer is take strategic violence as a method.*

Another student wrote, *The best method to bring freedom and security to Palestinians is the nonviolent method. By nonviolent method we highlight the justice in our case and stop the bleeding of both sides. For example, Oslo gave us lots what we wanted, but the violence of the second intifada took what we had and even more. Nonviolence shows that we are not terrorists because when you use the violence, you will be called a "terrorist" even if it's your right to use it. By using the nonviolent way, we don't give them the chance to do that. Nonviolence doesn't mean weakness or surrendering; on the contrary, it means that you have inner strength and perseverance. By that we will be respected in the outside world. Finally, nonviolence is the best method because all sectors of society will participate in the struggle against the enemy.*

Students began to think for themselves. In this collective Arab culture, students traditionally spoke on behalf of the whole class, saying, "We believe. . . ." I encouraged my students to speak for themselves, saying, "I believe" or "In my opinion."

We also wanted students to recognize other points of view. As students learned to listen to each other, they came to see the value in acknowledging ideas different from their own. Students in Peace and Conflict also wrote about this:

In my opinion, it's important to know other perspectives about peace and conflict. Because we live in the conflict and it's a part of our life, it's nice to discuss our problem and discuss which method is the best to solve our problem. When we listen to other opinions, maybe we will change our wrong perspectives. We benefit from other good perspectives. Also, we can convince each other about the best method that must be used to solve our problems.

Alongside the Peace and Conflict class, Jonathan and Susie, with others, established the Nonviolent Resistance Club. Students in the club learned that nonviolence does not mean being passive and that it is not a western or Christian ideology. Club members looked at examples of nonviolent activists in history, such as Mahatma Gandhi in India and Martin Luther King Jr. in the United States.

Students came to understand those who victimize them. In written dialogues and roleplays, students took the roles of Israeli soldiers or soldiers' families. They came to see that the Israeli is also a human being. This exercise helped them break down stereotypes.

In a later year, students moved a step further in understanding. Israeli peace activists came to campus to meet and collaborate with the club. Many AAUP students had never seen an Israeli without a gun. When students told their guests about Israeli army raids on their houses, the guests responded, "We believe everything you say." Not "Your reports are exaggerated," like Palestinians often heard when their stories were discounted.

A student told the club leaders after the meeting, "These Jews are amazing. I think they love peace even more than we do." This was unlike the oft-heard statement, "We Palestinians want peace, but the Israelis don't."

Many of our students thought the outside world did not understand or care about their plight. English Language Center teachers wanted them to know that others did care. In one class, students researched Israeli, Palestinian, and international organizations working to end the occupation. These included *Rabbis for Human Rights, Machsom Watch (The Checkpoint Women of Israel)*, the

International Solidarity Movement, Combatants for Peace, and Jewish Voice for Peace.

Becoming more articulate in English could help our students communicate more effectively with the international community. Describing their stories of mistreatment and humiliation in English could give them credibility and personal power.

My teachers created venues for students to express themselves. An email society paired our students with students in the U.K. and people from Palestinian support groups. In an online site named *Voices from Jenin*, our students posted narratives and poetry, sharing their stories with the larger world. These initiatives empowered students and connected them with others.

One year, the Nonviolent Resistance Club focused attention on boycotts. Led by Lasse, a language lab supervisor from Denmark, they studied successful boycotts in history, such as the bus boycott of the civil rights movement in the U.S. They researched how much money went from the West Bank to the Israeli economy and businesses through Tapuzina and Ein Gedi juices, soft drinks, and bottled water, all produced in Israel.

One student said, "We're buying the bullets that they are shooting on us." Another said, "We're supporting our enemy, paying for the weapons that oppress us."

The students then organized their own boycott of Israeli beverages, making posters and encouraging others to join in. Though the proposal was a new idea on campus and had only a small following, several years later, students would get AAUP to sign a formal agreement declaring a boycott of all Israeli-produced beverages on campus. The Nonviolent Resistance Club raised awareness about how students might take control of their own lives.

Some teachers had a special skill and unique passion for giving power to students. As their director, I felt proud of the way they took this responsibility to heart. Two years after I left Palestine, I would learn of the university-wide Israeli-made beverage boycott. This would remind me that we teachers do not always know the outcomes of our work. Our actions may have more far-reaching implications than we imagine. Maybe even Susie's prophetic words will come true in the future.

Susie wanted her Peace and Conflict class to understand that she was presenting ideas for students to think about. She did not seek to impose her own ideas on them. She told every group of students, "I am not Palestinian. I am not going to figure out the solution to this conflict. But one of you may. One of you may be a Palestinian hero someday because you may figure out how to solve this conflict."

20

Interfaith Relationships

"Are you a Christian or a Muslim?" a seven-year-old Muslim boy I knew was asked at his Christian school.

Puzzled by the question and wanting to fit in with his mostly Christian classmates, Mahdi shrugged his shoulders and said, "I am a Christian."

Mahdi's parents, good friends of mine in Nazareth, related the story to me. Though they were of Muslim background, they sent their young son to a Christian school in Nazareth, the town known as Jesus' childhood home. Attending Bible class was optional for Muslim children in the school, but Mahdi decided to attend. It was at the beginning of the year in the first Bible class that the teacher asked whether he was Christian or Muslim.

Some children are raised with a stronger sense of religious identity than Mahdi was. A young man I met in Zababdeh with a firm foundation in faith told me his story. His parents had named him Deen, which means "religion" or "faith" because religion and faith were so important to them. Deen's parents were devout Muslims. Since the age of five, Deen went with his father to the mosque for Friday prayers.

While Deen's parents raised him to follow the practices of Islam, they also exposed him to other faiths. They taught him that Judaism, Christianity, and Islam were similar and that it was good to know about all of them.

Deen reported to me, "When I was young, my parents took me to visit a church near our house. I started visiting the church often. I liked the icons and the candles. I noticed that Christians in the church said 'Amen' the same way Muslims in the mosque did. I thought we must be related somehow."

Deen continued, "In Jerusalem, my parents took me to the Western Wall, a holy site for Jews. At first, I laughed at the strange clothes and the bowing. I didn't know they were Jews. My father told me to stop laughing. He said, 'You shouldn't laugh at people who are praying. You should respect them.' I wondered why he wanted me to respect people who were occupying our country. My father explained the difference between politics and religion."

Deen learned the shared history, beliefs, and practices of the three monotheistic faiths: Judaism, Christianity, and Islam. All three trace their origins to Abraham. They share prophets, including Abraham, David, Solomon, and Elijah. In Islam, Jesus is considered a prophet, and Mary, his mother, is venerated. They all view God as Creator who is loving and gracious. Prayer and fasting are common practices. All three faiths preach compassion, justice, and peace.

Israel and Palestine are home to rich historical and religious sites. Some parts of Jerusalem as well as Rachel's Tomb near Bethlehem are considered sacred in all three faiths.

Bob and I visited many holy sites while living in Palestine. We traveled to Jerusalem, Bethlehem, Galilee, the Jordan River, Jericho, the Dead Sea, and Masada, among others. "Don't forget to bring your *joie de vivre,*" Bob said when we left the house. Then later, on site, he proclaimed, "Look where we are!"

"Look at these beautiful floor mosaics," I said, enchanted. My love of mosaics grew and grew.

Nablus, where Bob and I first met, is near ancient Shechem, where historically, Abraham first stopped in Canaan after leaving Iraq. Nablus is home to Jacob's Well, where biblical tradition says Jesus asked a Samaritan woman for water. One of the oldest churches in the world from the Byzantine era is built at the claimed site of Jacob's Well.

Another ancient church near AAUP stands in the small town of Burqin on the outskirts of Jenin. About twenty Christian families live in Burqin. St. George's Church, used by Greek Orthodox Christians, is where Jesus is said to have healed ten lepers on his way from Galilee to Jerusalem. Several Muslim students showed Bob and me around the tiny church, with its gold-painted icons, lanterns, and crosses. When Bob got out his flute, everyone sat down to listen, the acoustics flattering in the old stone structure.

Christians are a minority in both Israel and Palestine. In Israel, demographics are categorized ethnically, with about 75% Jews, 21% Arabs, and 4% other.[10] Of Palestinians living inside Israel, like young Mahdi in Nazareth, around 83% are Muslims, 9% are Christians, and 8% are Druze, a monotheistic, Arabic-speaking group.[11] Christians are concentrated in Nazareth.

In the West Bank, Christians are far fewer. The religious breakdown of the population is 1 to 2.5% Christian, 12 to 14% Jewish, and 80 to 85% Muslim.[12] Christians cluster in a few areas of the West Bank, like Bethlehem, Beit Sahour, Beit Jala, Ramallah, and our neighboring town, Zababdeh. The largest Christian groups are Greek Orthodox and Roman Catholics, while smaller groups include Melkite Greek Catholics and a variety of Protestants.

Tensions between Christians and Muslims occasionally arise. Christians sometimes face discrimination. At the university, some Muslim students verbally attacked a few Christian females for coming to campus in clothing they considered revealing. A group of Muslims attacked Christians for having a mixed gender party. There were disagreements about whether the cafeteria should be open or closed during Ramadan.

For the most part, however, Muslims and Christians at AAUP and in Palestine have good relations. When I asked people from both backgrounds about their interfaith relationships, they stressed their commonalities more than their differences. "We are all working together to fight the occupation," they often said.

Jonathan and a colleague established the Interfaith Dialogue Group at AAUP to promote understanding and respect among Christian and Muslim students. The Interfaith Dialogue Group gave students the chance to learn about each other's beliefs and understand their practices. About a dozen students met to hear each other's faith stories.

I welcomed opportunities myself to listen to others' stories of faith and share my own. I wanted to understand my Muslim colleagues and students, and I wanted them to understand me as a Christian.

The Interfaith Dialogue Group organized a work project for Muslim students in a small church in Zababdeh, with a positive response from the community. "Thank you for giving our children this chance to help Christians," Muslim parents told the leaders.

Christian students visited the mosque in Zababdeh and were equally grateful. "That was my first time to go inside a mosque," said one student. "Thank you."

The church in Burqin

Bob playing flute inside the church

Palestinian hospitality at Ibrahim's house

Cynthia and Bob's home—Michelle, Madalena, and Cynthia

Rooftop potluck with English teachers

Bob's students in a drawing class

Bob and students at Bob's art exhibition in Zababdeh

Bob's art exhibition at AAUP

Bob's art exhibition in Ramallah (*The Old City* on back wall)

Student demonstration with martyr poster at AAUP

Waleed congratulating Jonathan on two years of service

YEARS FOUR AND FIVE

Dear Human Being,

We know what the meaning of life is—that great thing that we haven't known for a long time. I hope that everyone who sees the light of the sun never sees the darkness of the hill that I live on. If you come to Palestine, you will admire the bounty of the flowers that cover this great land—my land, but you will be shocked by the destruction that follows you everywhere—the destruction that I must live with. Is this the life that a human being deserves? To see destruction and forget the beautiful flowers? I want to see life. I want to be a normal human. I want to be free.

—Student, Arab American University of Palestine

21

Soldiers, Everywhere

At 5:30 a.m. the walkie talkies beeped outside our bedroom window. Bob and I jumped out of bed to see a brown armored personnel carrier in one direction and a dark jeep in another. While I grabbed my camera and took a few shots from one of our windows, Bob picked up his camera and began taking shots from another. "How eerie," Bob murmured as he captured a picture of an Israeli soldier pointing his M-16 rifle directly at him.

The soldiers fanned out in the rocky hills for hours that day, shooting tear-gas canisters into small caves to flush out those they were searching for. They ransacked the tiny village of Tanin, just a quarter mile up the hill from our apartments, upturning large bags of flour, sugar, and rice stored up for the year.

What good does that do, I wondered, to destroy the food supply in a simple village without electricity?

In the late afternoon, they arrested two men on their wanted list and our local shepherd friend, Lateef. Lateef was questioned for several days before being released. It was not his first time in prison. Thousands of Palestinians were arrested during the first intifada and now, during the second.

The Israeli soldiers in the hills that day affected the mood on our campus. People wondered, What are they doing? Are they going to arrest students? A few hundred restless students gathered outside the College of Dentistry on the edge of campus. The security guards tried to keep them from throwing stones. Fakhree, the head of security, had a friendly face and the physique of a body builder. His prior experience in Group Seventeen, Yasser Arafat's personal team of bodyguards, had prepared him well for leading AAUP's twenty-man crew. He always seemed in control.

Having soldiers and students on the verge of a confrontation was a little too close for my comfort. But it helped me understand the reality of life in Palestine. Israeli soldiers, or *jaysh*, had become part of the landscape of our daily lives.

Sometimes, the *jaysh* drove into Palestinian towns and villages for no particular purpose. Palestinian kids might throw stones at the army vehicles, followed by the soldiers firing tear gas. Then the troops drove away.

One afternoon, Bob went to Zababdeh to pick up a few items from a small grocery store we frequented. On his way he walked by the taxi stand, the mechanic, the plastics shop, and a coffee shop where men played backgammon. Suddenly, everyone was running wild in the main road through town. Bob heard shooting and turned to see an Israeli jeep with a mounted machine gun at the far end of the road, along with four or five soldiers.

Tear gas appeared, smoke rising in the air, and Bob got a taste of its acrid fumes. It was suffocating; he could hardly breathe. His eyes were burning and began to water.

The young children in the street didn't know what was going on. One little boy, not more than three or four, saw Bob and with watering eyes said, "Hello." Parents hurried their children inside.

When Bob returned home, he didn't know what to think or how to report it to me. "They're just innocent little kids," he sighed. "My heart is breaking."

For this and other reasons, I had sleepless nights in Palestine. When I did sleep, I dreamed of violent encounters. I was under investigation, held hostage, and tortured. Jenin was a ghost town, and I was hiding out in a house. A Palestinian friend was executed in a stadium filled with people. An unidentified group tried to blow us up, Bob and me.

The background music of my dreams was the real-life noise of Israeli military vehicles, a constant in our life. In the stillness of the night, the vehicles thundered around in the fields like savage beasts. From several miles away, we heard roaring and growling in the hours of darkness.

The vehicles wreaked destruction. Tanks left their marks on the pavement of roads like ridges on a washboard. A tank could easily destroy a road with the heavy-duty hook attached to its back side that dug up the blacktop as the tank moved ahead. Armored personnel carriers were like tanks, but with soldiers holed up inside. Bulldozers built mounds and made trenches to hinder Palestinian movement. The earth was moved until a mound reached three or four feet. Anything less, and cars would manage to drive over it.

As often as the Israeli army moved dirt around, local Palestinians found other ways to get around. Their off-road tenacity and skill were like in a game of chess: "You block me here, and I'll go another route. You stop me there, and I'll find a way out." Bob and I called taxi drivers the heroes of Palestine because of their resolve to get people where they needed to go even if it seemed impossible. There is a joke told in the Arab world about Palestinians: *All Palestinians will get to heaven because they can always find a way.*

Some roads were blocked all the time, others only some of the time. The mounds and trenches changed constantly. West Bank Palestinians, whose vehicles had white or green license plates, were prohibited from all roads that led to Jewish settlements. Only Israelis and international passport holders with yellow-plated cars could use settler roads. Israeli soldiers at checkpoints protected settlements, settlers, and settler roads.

How to interact with checkpoint soldiers was not clear-cut. If we approached a checkpoint with our car too quickly, the soldier might yell, "Hey, slow down." If we drove too cautiously, the soldier might become annoyed and say, "Why are you going so slowly?" If we approached without being waved ahead, we were chastised, "Why did you come forward? I did not tell you to move. You do not come forward until I tell you to do so!"

One weekend morning, Bob and I were headed out to swim. To get to our destination, we would need to pass Jalameh checkpoint and the Green Line, the 1949 armistice line dividing the West Bank and Israel. We drove a white Peugeot 405, a car with yellow plates. But yellow plates did not guarantee access when the main routes were cut off. Coming to an intersection blocked by a mountain of dirt, we had to resort to off-road driving. We drove through dusty fields, hoping to get back onto the main road at some point.

Suddenly, we heard the roar of a moving armored personnel carrier. As the rumble got louder, we were sure they were after us. No other vehicles were in sight as we drove through the middle of a large field. We stopped the car immediately, our hearts beating fast. We looked at each other for a split second and asked, "What should we do? Stay in the car? Get out?"

We grabbed our passports, stepped out of the car, and held our hands up high in the air, as if we were under arrest. The armored personnel carrier continued towards us and came to an abrupt halt. The door on top was pushed open, and out came a soldier like a showgirl out of a cake. Within seconds, another soldier, then another, then one more appeared. I wondered how many were inside.

A soldier barked at us, "Where are you from?"

"America," we replied in chorus and handed him our passports.

"What are you doing here?" he asked, softening a bit.

"We teach at the university," I answered. He nodded his head, as if he knew of it.

"Where are you going?" he continued his interrogation.

"Ganhashlosha," I replied, using the Hebrew name for a natural spring called Sachne by Arabs. "We're going swimming."

For each place we went, there were two names, one Hebrew and one Arabic. Waleed had scolded me when I first arrived and was riding with him in his car. I had used the wrong name for a nearby city, Hebrew Beit Shean instead of Arabic Bisan.

A Palestinian friend's grandmother grew up in Bisan, but when the town was destroyed in 1948, the family moved close to Jenin. Israelis took over and renamed it Beit Shean, but Palestinians remember it as their town and use its Arabic name. The same goes for hundreds of towns and villages on the Israeli side of the Green Line.

I had learned from Waleed's rebuke that day that it would be to my advantage to use the Hebrew name when speaking to Jews and the Arabic name when speaking to Palestinians.

"You're not supposed to use this road," the soldier stated, referring to the settler road.

"But we've used it before, and it's quicker," I emphasized. "If we cannot use this road, it will take us more than an hour to get there."

The soldier agreed to let us use the settler road, which meant it would take only ten minutes to Jalameh checkpoint. However, we were unable to get our car over the bulldozed mounds to get onto the settler road. Though we were given permission, we had to turn back and drive one hour through Moonscape, the route winding through villages as well as fields that I had first encountered with the new teachers my second year.

Being chased by a military vehicle was a first. Usually, we approached *them*. When a gate was constructed a few months later to block all traffic from the settler road, I got out of the car, walked twenty or thirty feet up to and past the gate, and approached the soldiers in the tank nearby, asking permission to open the gate and use the road. Back in the U.S. in the future, it would feel strange to drive where I wanted.

At times like this, I remembered that there were Israelis who refused active duty in the West Bank. My own father had refused army duty during the Korean War in the 1950s, working in a hospital for two years instead. The Alternative Service Program gave conscientious objectors like my Mennonite father an alternative to bearing arms. Perhaps the Israeli conscientious objectors believed as Dad or I did—that there was a better way than military power.

We met different types of Israeli soldiers, both men and women. Some were gruff, others friendly. Some middle-aged, but many young. Some took a long time searching our passports just to remind us they could. Others found our visas quickly, handed back our passports, and said, "Have a nice day." Some said, "You must be crazy to work in Jenin." Others asked where we were from and chatted with us: "Oh, I've been to Virginia." "My uncle lives in Virginia." "Virginia, nice place." A jolly older soldier with a long white beard once said, "Thank you for choosing this checkpoint!"

It felt better to be treated kindly than not. Yet I knew Palestinians were not treated with the same respect. The words "Have a nice day" troubled me as I thought about life under occupation.

Even when soldiers disturbed me, I wanted to see them as human beings. Waleed and I argued about this. I said, "I hate what the soldier is doing, but I do not hate the soldier." He was skeptical of my desire to love my enemy.

I never knew what to expect with soldiers. My personal guideline was to be myself, to be friendly and honest, to stand up for my rights, and to advocate for the rights of Palestinians whenever I had the chance.

22

Political Activism

"Cynthia, a group of us are at a checkpoint," one of my teachers said in a midmorning call in September. "The Israeli soldiers are detaining some students. We feel we should stay and try to help, but our classes start in ten minutes. What should we do?"

"I'd like you to leave the checkpoint in time to teach your next class," I responded. "Some of your students will be expecting you."

The teachers were new to Palestine and new to The Situation. I could imagine their thoughts: We've got to do something! We can't stand by and do nothing! How can we teach when students are being held against their will? At the same time, our English program needed to run smoothly. In our situation, one's priorities could become confused.

One morning our help at a checkpoint was elicited. A Palestinian professor called me in my office, saying, "Cynthia, students are stuck on the other side of a pop-up checkpoint near Zababdeh, unable to pass through. Do you think you and some other teachers could go and pressure the soldiers to let the students pass?"

"I'll see what we can do," I replied.

A few minutes later, several of us were on our way. As our car rolled around the narrow curve and down the hill, kicking up dust, a mass of people came into view. We parked the car and walked through the crowd of a dozen faculty and a hundred or more students.

"What's going on?" I asked my colleagues.

"They're holding eight of our students. See them sitting on the ground over there?" We saw eight young men sitting on the road's edge, their hands tied behind their backs with plastic handcuffs. Israeli soldiers with guns hovered over them.

My colleagues and I walked up to the soldiers, hoping to persuade them to let the students pass. "Except for these eight on our list, everyone else is free to go. We already told the others they could pass," the soldier in charge affirmed.

We wandered through the throng of students, who explained, "As long as our brothers are here, we will stay. It is not right for us to leave them, even if the soldiers told us we can go. We will stand with our brothers no matter what." Their protest was calm and nonviolent. The solidarity was familiar to me by then, yet it still made an impression.

We walked back to the soldiers to see what we could do. "How long do you think it's going to take?" I asked the one in charge.

"We don't know. We are having some problems with our computer system, and we must wait until it is working to get the information we need about these young men."

"But they have exams that they should be taking right now," I insisted. We were in an exam period with a tight schedule.

The soldier's response carried no emotion. "Sorry, but there is nothing we can do. They will have to wait," he said and then repeated, "The others are free to go."

Some of us teachers turned back to return to campus. As we walked through the students, standing firm, they spoke the customary words of their litany: "This is our life. What can we do?"

Having religious or political interest was not a prerequisite to being hired at the Arab American University. Academic qualifications and teaching experience were more important than ideology. Each year as the recruiting team began interviewing candidates, I asked Waleed, "If we have to choose between a person who is qualified as an English teacher and one who is interested in Palestine, which shall we choose?" His answer was always the same: "Choose the one who is qualified as a teacher."

Some teachers had little or no knowledge of The Situation. One newly hired older man did not know where the West Bank was in relation to Gaza, Egypt, or Israel. He walked around greeting students, "Shalom," the Hebrew word for peace, not realizing the offense until I clued him in.

Some teachers had little or no political interest. A young teacher became furious with me one day when I knocked on his door to see if he wanted to engage with a group of students in the hall who had a political agenda. "Don't you ever do that again," he shouted at me. "I came here to teach, not to support a cause!"

Many of us did have interest in the Palestinian cause and advocated not only for our students and their country but also for peace when we could.

At the start of the U.S.-led war in Iraq, in March 2003, the English Language Center teachers made a poster in both English and Arabic: *Dear Students, We, your teachers from America, England, and Canada, do not support the invasion of Iraq. We do not support bombing Iraqis. This is an unjust action, and we are sorry it is happening.* Students stood around that day, reading the poster. As Jonathan walked into the cafeteria, students began clapping. "We are glad that you did not leave Palestine during the war," a student spokesman told him.

At a rally held on campus later that day, my Arabic speech echoed the words of our poster, and I added, "We are sad, but we are not alone in our sadness. Many people around the world are against this war. We are with you, and we will stay by your side even though our embassies have warned us to leave. We hope peace will come to Palestine, Iraq, and the whole world."

Some teachers spent much of their free time in political activities and advocacy. One weekend afternoon in the spring, I received a call from Susie, saying, "Cynthia, Lasse has been arrested." Lasse was Susie's Danish husband. Lasse was tall with straight, light hair that hung down past his ears. A gentleness wrapped round him—gentle eyes, gentle voice, big smile, listening ears.

Lasse, Susie, three other teachers, and two of our students were taking part in an anti-wall protest in the Palestinian village of Bil'in near Ramallah, along with one hundred or more internationals, Palestinians, and Israeli activists.

In June 2002, the Israeli government signed an agreement to build a barrier to prevent Palestinian attacks against Israelis. The barrier, made of electric fence, barbed wire, ditches and concrete up to thirty feet high, snaked around the West Bank and along the Green Line that separated Israel from the West Bank. The barrier, called a security barrier by Israel and a racial segregation wall or apartheid wall by Palestinians, separated many Palestinians from their farmland and pastureland. Bob and I saw this tragic wall when we visited Qalqilya, Bethlehem, and other places.

Bil'in was the site of weekly demonstrations against the Israeli occupation and separation barrier. Lasse joined the demonstrations, taking students from the Nonviolent Resistance Club. He thought it would inspire students to see their own Palestinian people actively resisting the occupation.

Lasse was arrested for refusing to move from the ground where he stood with a Palestinian flag in hand. He asked the Israeli soldier to show him the required documentation stating that the land where he was standing was a closed military zone. Instead, the soldier took him into custody. After two days in prison and a court hearing, Lasse was released.

While Lasse was in prison and we were waiting to get more information, Susie came to my apartment and recounted the story. "I feel so bad for Lasse," I sighed. "And I wish I had been there with you. I haven't gone to any of the demonstrations in Bil'in," I bemoaned, down on myself.

Susie looked at me and said, "Cynthia, your life is one long demonstration."

Back in September, when my teachers had asked about staying at the checkpoint, I called a meeting with Waleed, hoping he could clarify our priorities. Waleed gave an overview of the situation, and then teachers asked questions. After their questions, I had one: "If a teacher has class and there is a checkpoint situation such as the one this morning, what should the teacher do?"

I expected Waleed to advise teachers to go to class, so his answer surprised me. He stated, "It could help for teachers to be at the checkpoint."

The fact that Waleed said the opposite of what I was expecting revealed the ambiguity with which we lived. There was never one answer because of the confusing nature of The Situation. One thing was clear—that the occupation affected our students, their families, and every aspect of institutional life.

23

Living in Isolation

On the edge of campus in the middle of the countryside, we lived in virtual isolation. The small communities of Talfit and Tanin were the only villages nearby. Zababdeh was a mile away. Our work, visiting, activism, and walks took place in the light of day. We had nowhere to go at night except the Zaytouna restaurant.

It was risky to travel after dark. The military *jaysh* could appear anytime, anywhere. The chance of getting shot was real. To stay safe, Palestinians in our area did not venture out much at night.

In an earlier year, I hadn't realized how confining rural life was until I went to Ramallah after a long stretch on the hill. I'm in heaven, I thought, to be out after dark in a city with a cultural scene.

In Jenin, no bookstores sold literature in English. Bob and I both loved to read and grabbed any book we could find. One Christmas holiday, we went to Jerusalem for the weekend. After an hour in a bookstore, Bob smiled and said to me, "You look so happy in here."

My teachers left their jobs, in part, due to the isolation. Even people who loved solitude found our solitude difficult to bear. We had to make our own fun. "I want you to make me laugh today," Bob said, giving me my one weekend task.

We studied our maps and shared places we would like to go. A map of Israel and Palestine was posted behind our front door; a world map hung near our bedroom. "What are your top five dream countries?" Bob asked me one day.

"What are yours?" I asked him.

"You can't answer a question with a question!" he teased.

When English-language movie channel MBC 2 was added to our cable TV, I found myself watching movies I would never think of watching back home. "*Men in Black* is on tonight," Bob announced after dinner.

"Great! Let's watch it!" I said. The screen was small, but that did not matter.

Sometimes, friends joined the movie watching. A neighbor brought her two-inch pet turtle. When the turtle came to visit, it crawled up our arms and legs. We fed it lettuce and cucumber.

Mice took us away from the maps, the turtle, and the TV. I kept a record each time we spotted, trapped, or killed a mouse in the Era of the Mice. I named them Mr. Mouse One, Mr. Mouse Two, Mr. Mouse Three. While the mice next door stayed out of sight, our mice were audacious.

"One is peering right at me," I exclaimed when I opened our closet door. There on a shelf sat a mouse on top of a stack of folded clothes.

"It's staring at me from the counter," Bob told me as he worked at his computer one night. "How do the mice get all the way up here?" he added. We lived on the third floor.

One mouse scampered across the living room carpet while the TV was on. Another scraped behind the kitchen cupboard as we sat and listened. Yet another jumped from the stove to the counter and ate cilantro from a tiny metal plate while Bob observed from the sofa. One rooted around in a laundry basket in our bedroom when we were in bed.

Bob became an expert at isolating a mouse to a certain area of a room and then trapping it under our blue plastic wash tub, prattling to the rodent as I hopped around and squealed. In another instance, we chased a furry little creature down the polished stairway of our building, watching it scurry and then skip a few stairs, jumping to the next level of tiled landing. When we were near the bottom landing, the mouse got spooked. Instead of dashing outside the open door and into the field as we had hoped, he raced back up the steps in front of our eyes, probably into our apartment, which he considered home. Two neighbors came to watch one time during the Era of the Mice.

Neighbors also gathered on Game Night. I learned to play poker, bidding with toothpicks. We made up crazy names for each round. Scrabble games were recorded in my Scrabble notebook—what we ate, the words formed, and the quotes of the night. One friend dazzled us with her seven-letter words. Another wowed us with his tight two- and three-letter grids. My Scrabble skills, I realized, were limited. Bob joked, "What am I doing playing Scrabble with English teachers?" Yet Bob and I kept at it. When a friend of mine visited from the U.S., one of our game partners joined us for a round of Scrabble. That is how we showed off our life in Palestine.

Bob and I played not only Scrabble but also backgammon and cribbage. Bob was new to backgammon, so I taught him what I knew from my Egypt days. We opened the board after dinner, saying, "The loser washes the dishes!" Cribbage, a favorite game in the Gravelin family, became a favorite of ours. "You're feeling lucky, aren't you?" Bob said as we sat down to play.

Another teacher and I played a different sort of game. We listed the ways we could tell that we had been in Palestine a long time: *When you walk on the streets instead of the sidewalks. When you refer to your home country as America rather than the United States. When you call female students girls instead of women. When you say "Insha Allah," meaning God willing, at the end of every sentence. When you use expressions in English that your students use: "As you like," "Please close the lights," and "I love you too much." When you hear loud explosive sounds from outside and continue with what you are doing. When a student says he was in prison, you give a brief acknowledgment and then go on with your class. When driving in places outside of Palestine, you take the dirt path instead of the paved road.*

Our Murder Mystery Dinner was good fun also, but Jenin Jam Sessions were even more lively. In one or another campus apartment, Bob and others made music with guitars, harmonicas, egg shakers, and Arabic drums. I often joined in. When this group of teachers living near a war zone in the middle of nowhere let our feelings flow, tunes of all types emerged. We improvised rock, jazz, blues, gospel, country, folk, and bluegrass, sometimes one clear style and other times a jumble. With lyrics springing from one person to another, we created *Catfish and Beans; Prance, Prance, Prance, All the Way to France; Before She Falls Again;* and *Checkpoint Blues,"* singing about everything and nothing at the same time. When the evening grew late and the lyrics died down, a percussion jam followed. The silliness mellowed into a guitar instrumental that mirrored the stillness of the Palestinian countryside. Nothing compared to jamming.

Bob's musical performances at the university and Zababdeh's Latin Patriarchate School entertained not only us but others. Harried voices became hushed as the melodies of Bob's flute floated through the performance hall, as the rhythms of the drum spoke their secrets. "Thank you for showing us something different," said students and community people alike.

Bob shared his paintings at the same venues and later in Ramallah. Entitled *Soulscapes, Expressions,* and *I See What I See,* Bob's shows were a diversion in an atmosphere enveloped by The Situation and void of extracurricular activities. Stepping into his exhibits was like entering another world. As people shook Bob's hand or wrote guest book comments, they uttered, "Beautiful images." "What does it mean?" "That's how *I* am feeling."

Some of Bob's works would find a home in Palestine: *The Old City, Wildflowers, The Occupation, String Theory, The Visitors, In Fields at Play, Yellow and Blue.* Having paintings in Palestine would keep Bob connected even after leaving. Years later, while working in Kuwait and watching the evening news on Iran's Press TV, our eyes would grow large as we saw a painting of Bob's on the TV screen. The news reporter was doing an interview in the Ramallah hotel lobby where Bob's seven-foot high painting, *The Old City,* was hung. "It's your painting!" I cried out as the news story played on.

"Who would have thought?" Bob smiled.

24

Intimidation at the Border

When Israeli immigration officials prohibited Jonathan and another teacher from entering Israel in November 2003, it affected all of us on campus. Their students wondered if they would be alright. With 1,000 students to attend to in our fourth year, I wondered how we would cover their classes. Other international faculty wondered if the same fate awaited them on their upcoming visa renewal trips. We all wondered when our friends would return. As it turned out, one never did, and Jonathan had to wait two months in Jordan before he was permitted to enter Israel.

Just as Israeli soldiers stationed at checkpoints throughout the West Bank had power over our mobility, Israeli immigration officials at border entry points held our lives in their hands. We lived apprehensively.

In my first year at AAUP, the Israeli government granted work permits, but those were given in tandem with an official tourist visa which lasted only three months. Visa renewal trips were a part of our life. In my five years of work, I traveled out of Israel and back into Israel twenty-seven times to renew my visa. I facilitated visa renewals for my teachers as well.

Some renewals took place at Ben Gurion Airport in Tel Aviv when coming back from the States after summer holiday. Most visa runs, however, involved traveling 120 miles to Amman, Jordan one day and crossing back into Israel the next.

When we left Israel, we had to pay a departure tax, answer questions asked by Israeli security, have our bags searched, wait for a bus to drive us several hundred meters to the Jordanian side of the border crossing, and go through immigration procedures and baggage check on the Jordanian side.

The trip required the services of three taxis. A West Bank Palestinian took us from the university to Jalameh checkpoint in a white-plated vehicle. A Palestinian living inside Israel with yellow plates on his car transported us from the Israeli side of the checkpoint to "the bridge," or border crossing between Israel and Jordan. A Jordanian moved us from the Jordanian side of the bridge to a hotel in Amman.

On a good day, we left the university after class at 3:00 p.m. and reached Amman by 7:00 in the evening. On a bad day, security and immigration procedures took four or five hours, extending the total trip up to eight hours.

One time, five of us American and Canadian teachers sat together in a drab waiting area with tourist posters of Israel on the walls. Young Israeli security personnel checked and re-checked our bags. They examined Arabic language notes, playing cards, cosmetics, and undergarments. I tried to distract myself by reading or talking with colleagues, but my attention kept coming back to the examining table. How often will they handle the things in our bags? I wondered.

Bob and I usually welcomed a day or two in Amman. Regular breaks from life on the hill helped us keep our sanity. But not knowing how we would be treated upon our return nor whether we would be allowed back in added a nervous edge to our weekends away.

The odds seemed to be against us. After watching the people in front of us glide smoothly through security, we would be singled out and held for questioning. Sometimes, we ran out of patience.

"Why am I always the one you choose to interrogate?" Bob snapped, out of character. "Why don't you pick on someone else?" He was raising his voice at an Israeli official much younger than him with wavy hair and dark eyes. The official wore the standard navy-blue pants and light gray shirt with a walkie talkie dangled over his shoulder.

The security official asked Bob to take a seat on a bench about ten feet away. He then turned to me and asked in a condescending tone, "Why do you think your husband is so upset?"

Knowing that the official had the power to deny our entry, I answered coolly while masking my emotions, "Because every time we come through here, we are made to wait and to answer the same questions. We watch other people walk right through. We are just teachers who want to teach. We get tired of going through this. I'm sure you can understand."

"I'm sorry for the inconvenience, but we are just trying to do our job," the security officer replied, cold and business-like.

I heard that line more than one time. I also knew their tactics. No matter the border crossing, the officials were trained to repeat the same questions again and again, sometimes rephrasing them. Maybe we would slip up and get caught in a lie.

"You already asked me twice why I chose to work in Jenin, and I already answered your question twice!" Bob raged at a male-female duo at the Tel Aviv airport. "How many times are you going to ask me the same question?"

"Sir, we have our procedures to follow. We are just doing our job. Getting upset is not going to help you get on that airplane more quickly."

I intervened, "Could you direct your questions to me?"

They agreed and continued to plod through their inquiries about our jobs, residence, marriage, friends, and financial situation until they were satisfied that we did not pose a threat to the security of the state of Israel.

It took hours at Ben Gurion International Airport each time I left on a recruiting trip or summer visit to the States. I became used to the routine. I rarely flinched no matter how many questions I was asked, how long my bags were examined, or how thoroughly my body was searched. While the female security officers asked me to pull down my jeans so they could flicker their magic wand around my crotch, I tried to think of them as human beings who had hobbies, favorite foods, and people they loved. I complied with whatever they asked. They usually uttered an unemotional apology before and after the body searches, and I strangely thanked them at the end. I could finally come down from my heightened state of awareness as I sat in the modern airport terminal, the water of a large fountain tumbling down from the ceiling. I loosened up even more once seated on the plane.

When returning to Israel, I was often told, "You cannot keep coming in and out like this. You cannot work on a tourist visa. You have to go to the Israeli Ministry of the Interior to get a work visa."

In the early years, I responded, "The university has applied for work permits, and we are still waiting." In later years, after the breakdown in cooperation between the Israeli government and the Palestinian Authority, I stopped mentioning work permits and just answered, "I know."

The immigration officials said, "You cannot keep doing this" but then went ahead and stamped a tourist visa in my passport each time. I did not care that they sometimes crossed out *three months* and replaced it with *one month* or *two weeks*. I was always happy to make it into the country even if I had to leave again in two weeks.

Thousands of internationals were working in the West Bank, and as I understood it, very few if any had been granted work visas. It was a Catch-22 situation. The border authorities said we had to get work visas from the Ministry of the Interior, yet the Ministry of the Interior did not grant visas to people working inside the West Bank. Bob calculated how much money the Israeli government was making off internationals living in the West Bank who paid a departure tax on every visa run.

If nothing else, it made for great story telling. Each of us teachers had our own dramatic portrayals of our entries into Israel. A few teachers had more drama to recount than I, with computers confiscated, full-body searches, and a thirteen-hour interrogation. Some teachers thought they had figured out why Israeli security personnel said this or did that.

The longer I stayed in Palestine, however, and the more we traveled in and out, the more I believed that our legal status was not something to figure out. The system was arbitrary, changeable, and dependent in part on the mood of the border official each time. Though some officials seemed intent on intimidation, harassing us with their probing questions, others seemed innocent in doing their jobs. No matter what their motivations, I did my best to not be intimidated.

25

Death is all Around

Palestinian martyr posters were everywhere. Plastered on shop fronts and the sides of buildings in Zababdeh and Jenin, the posters pictured the dead Palestinian wielding a gun with Jerusalem's Dome of the Rock in the background. At the university, students made their own posters and displayed them across campus, offering condolences to those who had been killed defending their country. They wrote in Arabic, *Glory and eternity to our martyrs, the good ones.*

Yasser Abu-Laimoun's poster appeared on campus the day after he was killed in April 2004, the university's fourth year. He was the second AAUP faculty member to be killed by Israeli forces. Dr. Khalil Suleiman had been the first, killed two years earlier in his ambulance in Jenin Refugee Camp.

Yasser, a lecturer in Hospital Administration, had come to AAUP the previous year from the U.S., where he received his master's degree. Rather than settling in Zababdeh, as some faculty did, he lived in his home village, Taluza, twenty miles away, wanting to be with his extended family.

Yasser was shot dead on a weekend while walking in a field, taking lunch to his sister tending the crops. At age thirty-three, he left behind a twenty-one-year-old wife, a young daughter, and a second daughter on the way. Israeli soldiers had been in the village looking for two activists of Hamas, a militant Palestinian political party. The Israeli military admitted one week later that Yasser Abu Laimoun was not a "terrorist" and that his shooting had been a mistake. Waleed, quoted in a New York Times article, stated, *I'm sure it is not enough for the family*, referring to the admission of error.

Virtually every person at the university had faced the death of a relative or friend. Each year we grieved countless losses. But that academic year, 2003-2004, seemed particularly horrific. More deaths than usual impacted our campus community, and more deaths touched me than at any other time in my life. A student's poem summed it up:

Maybe the birds are free to fly
Maybe the flowers are free to grow
But we are just free to die
In this land called Palestine

A white owl with yellow eyes appeared on campus that year, remaining for several days. It perched on a tree that Bob and I passed on our walk from home to work. We had not seen that owl type before, and it seemed out of place. The owl is viewed as a harbinger of death in some cultures. Did the owl show up because of the deaths? we wondered.

Palestinian deaths at the hands of the Israeli military were unspeakable. A twelve-year-old girl was killed in an army attack in her Jenin school where a friend of mine was the principal. Two young sons of an older AAUP student were shot one afternoon along a street in their village, Al-Judeida. Their father, Abdel Moneim, a brother to Ibrahim, related the story to Bob and me when we visited his home. The boys had been walking to buy bread for the family when bullets came out of nowhere and ended their young lives. Bilal was ten years old, and Ashraf was eight. During our visit, we looked at Bilal and Ashraf's photographs displayed under glass in a large frame on the living room wall. Our hosts were expecting a new baby boy and planned to name him after one of his brothers. I would learn later that the village school was also named after the boys.

With each death, there was a story—the story of the person's life and the story of the person's death. In some cases, I had a personal connection. I had shared an office hall with Yasser, and we had chatted on occasion. He was always looking out for the best interests of his students and was serious about his job. Yasser believed that classes should not be cancelled whenever someone was martyred. He thought that strength and resistance were more visible when students kept on studying. After his death, I sat in remembrance with others in the business college where he had taught. A student of Yasser's wrote a tribute to him (adapted):

> *I always believed in Khalil Gibran's quote which says, "You give but little when you give of your possessions. It is when you give of yourself that you truly give." This quote reminds me of Yasser Abu Laimoun because he was an example in giving. He was not only our teacher, but he was also our guide, friend, and brother. . . . Why did they kill him? Was it because of his message in life? His message was education, honesty, and good manners. It was academic oriented. Or did they punish him because he taught us how to love life and never give up hope whatever the situation? . . .*

Some deaths were natural deaths yet connected to The Situation. The mother of my friend and colleague, Leen, died of a brain tumor. What made her mother's death unnatural was the fact that neither Leen nor her sisters could see their mom before she died because of travel restrictions placed on them as Palestinians. While her mother lay dying in a hospital in Amman, Jordan, where she had gone to seek treatment, Leen tried unsuccessfully to gain permission from the Israelis to travel. "This is life," Leen said to me.

In her place, I visited Leen's unconscious mother. I tried to speak for Leen. "Leen loves you," I whispered. "Leen is here with you in spirit." I held her hand in my own and watched her body systems shutting down, monitored by a machine.

In Leen's place, I sat with her father in the hospital cafeteria before his wife died. He said, "She was a good woman and a good teacher. She was always giving. She was always doing something for others. Now we are waiting for God to relieve her suffering. There is nothing we can do." He broke down when Leen's brother showed me photos of his mom.

Fatal car accidents on the road connecting Zababdeh to the university ended the lives of two of our own: Nasser Khuzameyya, a staff member in his late twenties, and a young male student. The deaths were an indirect result of the Israeli occupation. With the failing Palestinian economy and lack of funds, roads were only narrowly paved, making it difficult to pass or drive safely. The university's attempt to make that narrow road safer by putting in speed bumps had failed to prevent the deaths.

Nasser, the staff member killed on the road, was one of the first people I met when I arrived at the university back in 2000. As a security guard, he was on duty in the entrance hall of the main administrative building where I had my office. When I left work in the early evening, I often found Nasser reading a newspaper or a book, which stood out to me. Nasser was always ready for a conversation, and I used to stop by for a chat. He was interested in asking about me and my life, which was also unusual. The day Nasser died was his first day in a new position in the Student Affairs division. He would have had so much to offer our students, I thought. But a poorly built road with a sharp curve took his life instead.

While Bob went to Nasser's burial, as was appropriate for only men to do, I sat in his home the next day with mourning women. Most of the furniture had been removed and replaced by white plastic chairs lined against each wall. Nasser's mother, dressed in black and clutching a tissue in her hand, repeated aloud her litany of lament, "They said he was okay. They said it was only a broken leg." But internal bleeding had taken his life.

Nasser's young wife clung to their newborn baby boy, bundled in a blanket in her arms. She stared straight in front of her. Their young daughter, with big dark eyes and curly black hair, came home from nursery school and went to her mother's knees, smiling. "Your daddy is in paradise," she had been told.

Nasser said to me in our last conversation before his car accident, "How is it possible that you have lived here more than three years and have never visited my home like your husband has?"

I wondered the same and answered, "I would like to. Let's arrange it." Regrettably, I never got the chance.

After each death occurred, I sat with a roomful of women as they shared their sorrow. I thought of my Yoder grandparents who had run a funeral home, helping in the time of grief. Grandma always said to her son, my father, "It was his time. It was her time."

In Palestinian tradition, women gather to mourn for three days in the home of the one who died while men gather outside or in another location. I shed tears with women I knew and women I had never met. "Can you tell me about your loved one?" I asked. "Can you show me a photograph?"

I drank bitter coffee with the other mourners, as sugar is not served around death. I sat quietly and listened to the cries of anguish and expressions of faith: *"Allah yarhamu,"* May God have mercy on his soul; *"Allah yarhamha,"* May God have mercy on her soul; *"Alhamdulillah,"* Thanks be to God.

I learned to offer words of sympathy according to the culture: *"Al-baqi fi hayatik,"* May the rest of his or her life be lived in yours; *"Azama Allah ajrukum,"* May God reward you; *"Allah ma'akum,"* May God be with you.

As the year progressed, other deaths continued. At the same time, several friends had babies or became pregnant. Leen was pregnant with her second child when her own mother died in the hospital in Jordan. I thought about life ending and life beginning.

As the winter rains ended and the ground dried up, I resumed my morning walks in the hills. I observed with more wonder than ever before the vast display of wildflowers: white and yellow daisies and chamomile, lavender irises, pink cyclamen, rich red anemones and poppies, silver sea quills, deep purple thistles, and blue cornflowers. I watched their cycle of blooms, a cycle of life and death. Thank you, God, I prayed, for this reminder to cherish the beauty of all that is alive around me.

26

Turkeys from Talfit

The women at the wedding party of my friend Aisha's seventeen-year-old niece knew how to let loose. The men were not around, so spaghetti-strap dresses bared shoulders, neck lines exposed cleavage, slit skirts revealed thighs, and hair was uncovered. It was my first time to see Aisha's hair. The women danced to the rhythm of the music in this house rid of its furniture. It was like a night club, but with Arabic songs. Another teacher and I joined in the laughter and dancing. We drank sickly sweet Cola and shouted over the noise. We congratuled the young bride, *"Mabruk, mabruk!"* How wonderful to be part of this celebration, I thought.

I was invited to take part in a different kind of celebration by another friend, Widad. In Islamic tradition, on special occasions like the birth of a baby or a high school graduation, sheep are slaughtered. Widad, a single mother of three school-aged daughters, had a sheep slaughtered to honor and celebrate the life of another friend's father, who had recently passed away.

Widad, her friend, and I watched as the hired butcher slaughtered, skinned, and eviscerated the sheep on the small porch of Widad's Jenin home. Our fleece jackets kept us warm, and we kept our distance from the blood. The butcher then cut the meat into fist-sized chunks, while we filled thirty plastic bags with an equal amount of meat each. It was common practice when slaughtering an animal to give one-third to the poor and another third to one's relatives and to keep one-third for one's own family. With the recipient list in hand, we piled into Widad's small car and drove around the city, delivering the meat to each household. We then returned home to make our own dinner. Widad loved to cook, and her daughters often helped. They were always inviting women into their home.

"Thank you for letting me be with you today," I said to Widad before leaving.

"No, thank you for being with us," she replied. I always had a home away from home at Widad's house.

I became so enamored with sheep that by the time I left Palestine, I had collected fourteen sheep skins to give to my nieces, nephews, and friends in the U.S. I spread the fluffy white skins across the living room floor one evening just to look at them. Sheep and olive trees meant life to the people of Palestine.

For Palestinians, olive trees are a symbol of their connection to the land carried from one generation to another. Bob and I picked olives with our friends each fall, joining the family affair on weekends or in the late afternoon after work. The first time, I felt like a delighted child. *"Masha Allah*—This is great!" I raved as we whacked the tree branches with sticks. "Listen to that pitter patter!" I enthused as the hard, ripe olives fell onto the white, green, or blue tarps spread on the ground below. If sticks were in short supply, we lifted our arms and picked the olives from off the trees directly. We then scooped the green olives up from the tarp or ground and placed them in large, sturdy bags. "Look at all these olives!" I exclaimed.

We joked and chatted while we worked, giving Bob and me a chance to practice Arabic. We wore jeans and T-shirts, while our women friends from the village wore long, traditional dresses.

After a few hours of hard work, we sat down on the ground or a tarp in the shade, sipped tea, and ate flatbread dipped in olive oil and fresh thyme, called *zeit wa zaatar* in Arabic. Smiles and laughter joined us.

Palestinians depended on olives for economic livelihood, and they were proud of their harvest. Those who collected olives for landowners received part of the yield in exchange for their labor. Friends in their villages took us to the local olive press. There we watched as the huge bags of fruit were dumped into the machine that ground them and turned them into a thick gold-green liquid. Our hosts explained, "We bring our own bottles and fill them up for the year." In homes, we were shown the year's store—a couple hundred two-liter soda bottles each of oil and preserved fruit. Sometimes, we received priceless gifts of olives, olive oil, grape jam, or honey.

In faculty housing, sharing food was the norm. I made and delivered my standard goodies: peanut butter fingers, apple cake, strawberry jam, or pear cream pie. Just as often, I was on the receiving end. Homemade bread came from Chelle in Apartment S-3, pancakes with apple topping on the weekend from Chieko in Apartment F-6, soups and stews from Michelle in S-1 and Zarqa in F-3, and stuffed zucchini or *maftul*, rolled wheat served with broth, from the mother of a Palestinian professor next door.

My second year at AAUP, the year Bob was gone, nothing made my day more than Chieko's notes under my door after work: *We have chicken curry tonight. If you want to enjoy it with us, welcome! Tonight, we have peanut soup, rice, and bread. If you are hungry, come to our house!*

For Thanksgiving and Christmas, we ordered turkeys from Hisham in Talfit, and guests brought the trimmings. "It's green!" our friends yelped as they walked in the door where the stove stood just to the right. I had followed a suggestion from *The Joy of Cooking*. I had covered the Talfit turkey with a damp cloth soaked in oil to hold in the moisture while roasting. What I had not realized when I chose a green kitchen towel was that the dye could leak into the fowl drippings in the roaster pan. That night, though cautious, we covered our mashed potatoes in green gravy.

One Christmas, we had a white elephant gift exchange. What a great chance to share gifts we've received, I thought. We teachers showed off our gifts in our offices, comparing degrees of uniqueness. A miniature wooden model of an Israeli tank, when wound up, rotated its barrel around and played the theme song from *Love Story*. Two hands with long red fingernails held a heart-shaped porcelain clock. A ceramic pen holder stuck to a model who had blond hair, a miniskirt, and knee-high boots. Stuffed animals, stuffed hearts with *I Love You,* fake flowers, and picture frames with imaged edges decorated teachers' desks. Glass or cloth maps of Palestine stood on shelves or hung on walls.

Instead of a gift exchange, I liked to greet guests with a warm flannel lentil bag placed around the back of their neck, a gift idea from my older sister many years before. On one occasion, Samah and Leen helped me warm the bags in the microwave. Palestinian friends often joined get-togethers, but a turkey meal was a first for my two assistants at work. A potluck was also a first. In our kitchen, Leen and Samah helped mash potatoes and carve the bird. What a nice switch, I thought, from my always asking Palestinian friends how to make dishes. "Oh, what did you bring?" Samah and Leen asked as guests arrived with their foods.

The lentil bags, oven warmth, and twenty people in our small living room filled the chilly apartment with heat. The plant on the TV served as Christmas tree. White lights and a string of red chili peppers framed the lone window. After dinner, we sang Christmas songs with Bob on guitar. "Thank you for printing the words so we could sing too," Samah cheered. "It was such a nice evening."

"The turkey was delicious, and so were the sweets," praised Leen. "This Christmas party was amazing."

One of the things I loved about Palestine was that limited space did not stop people from gathering. In the U.S., I may have heard, "We don't have enough room." "How could we fit enough chairs?" "No way, it wouldn't work." In small spaces in Palestine, there was always room.

Celebrating traditions together made me feel that life was normal after all. One January, I received a letter from a friend in the States, telling me what she had baked and bought over the holidays, and what her children had done. At the end she wrote, *This is all very shallow news compared to life in Palestine.* On the contrary, I thought, the little things in life are what matter.

27

Reflection at Graduation

My heart swelled as students walked across the stage and received their diplomas. Parents and family members in the audience beamed with pride. I was beaming too. The university had made it to this momentous first graduation. We did it.

It was a June evening in 2004. A balmy breeze blew, barely keeping us cool. Smells of the desert mixed with the varied aromas of the guests in attendance. The sunset call to prayer in nearby Talfit had not yet sounded; village animals were quieting down. Students and faculty wearing bluish-gray gowns with black stripes sat near the stage, a sea of deep gray blending into the sky's dark hues.

That evening my mind went back over four years. I saw students parked eagerly in the front row of class and students slouched sleepy in back. I recalled discussions in classrooms and hallways and the insights I had gained. I pictured students' homes, families, villages, and dreams for the future as I continued my reverie.

My thoughts moved to The Situation and the heart-wrenching stories I had heard or witnessed. Yet the resilience of the Palestinian people shone through that night at graduation. I could hear them saying "*Haik al-haya.* This is life."

Jim Thomas, Senior Advisor to the President the first two years, returned from Utah for the special event. It felt so good to give him a big hug. In his speech, Jim said, "It has been an honor to be part of this fine university's development. I believe the university will have many great achievements in the future." He then spoke to the graduates, many of whom already had jobs lined up: "Congratulations to each of you. I encourage each one of you to contribute to your families and to Palestine in the future."

Waleed Deeb, Founding President, spoke of the university as a national project, asking those assembled to protect and support it as such. "It is an institution for you, your children, and your grandchildren," he said. "It will benefit this community and the nation."

Both men had been key to the university's success. I looked at the faculty that night seated in their regalia and felt grateful to be part of this endeavor, to work with an amazing array of people.

I stayed one more year after that. Year Five saw more than 4,000 students at AAUP. We taught English to over 1,000. The language center moved to a new, bigger space. Our team kept growing—sixteen faculty, six lab supervisors, and our two administrative staff. We traveled to Birzeit University and Bethlehem University to meet with other English teachers. We led two external projects—a professional development program with high school teachers and a micro-scholarship program with high school students, both with funding from abroad.

While many things were new, more things were the same:

More students to know, paragraphs to read, and classroom moments to savor. More teachers to interview and try to keep happy. More chaos on campus and sometimes calm.

More walks and talks with Waleed. More admiration as he faced challenges: students in Israeli prisons, faculty becoming politicized, students turning to violence, guns on campus, the lack of law and order, threats against Waleed. Despite the heat, Waleed kept on believing that education can transform lives.

More strolls in Jenin for Bob and me. More wandering in the hills. More stones from the land to add to our collection of treasures.

More entertaining ourselves in old and new ways. More olive picking and engagement parties. More shared meals with friends.

More visa runs and checkpoint soldiers.

More sadness at violence on both sides.

More listening to stories and pain to share. More aches in our heads and hearts.

More tenacity and determination to witness as we saw Palestinians under occupation living their lives.

Every year Bob and I asked ourselves, "How long shall we stay? Will this be our last year?" It was hard to stay but would also be hard to leave.

On the one hand, we did not want to leave jobs we enjoyed, a land we found beautiful, and the people we loved, especially the people we loved.

At the same time, The Situation was wearing, and we did not know how much more we could take. We felt good about what we had accomplished at the university in both English and art, so maybe it was alright to let go.

We weighed the pros and cons, which seemed about evenly balanced, and we finally made the difficult decision to leave.

Waleed, Bob, and I left our jobs at the university at the end of Year Five. Waleed carried on with The Young Scientists Club, thinkshops, and new critical thinking endeavors in both Palestine and Jordan. Bob and I transitioned to Ramallah for a few months where Bob continued painting and showing his work. He was also hired by the Museum without Borders to photograph Islamic art in Jerusalem. My special project begun the previous year kept me connected to AAUP and the other partners—Educational Testing Service in the U.S. and the Palestinian Ministry of Education—for one more semester.

We were scheduled to leave Palestine in January 2006, five and a half years after we had first arrived. One month prior to our departure date, we had our belongings shipped from Israel to the U.S. The day the shipping company arrived to collect our things, the elevator in our Ramallah apartment building stopped working, a first since we had moved in. As we carried our items down three flights of stairs, going down and back up many times, we wondered if that was a sign. Maybe we were not supposed to leave.

We did leave Palestine the following month, but we carried the memories of our Palestinian friends with us.

28

A Reminder

Nearly everyone living in Palestine has a travel tale to tell. One of mine would remind me, even years later, what life can be like for Palestinians who live in the West Bank.

The special project I was part of took me back and forth between Jenin and Ramallah for several months at the end of my Palestinian experience. Traversing rocky paths, pot-holed paths, muddy paths, or no paths at all to get to a destination was a routine part of my life.

It was 1:00 p.m. on a December afternoon when I set out on the seventy-five-mile trip from Jenin to Ramallah in a shared taxi van, along with six university students. We were picked up in Zababdeh, eight miles south of Jenin. The students were going home for the three-day holiday, *Eid Al-Adha,* the Islamic Feast of the Sacrifice, which commemorates Abraham's willingness to sacrifice his son Ishmael in obedience to God.

The students chatted with me a bit and then became quiet. Maybe they were thinking of what their mothers would cook or who they would see back home. I settled into my seat in the front beside the driver, Saleem, a hefty man who liked to talk but took his job as a driver seriously. He had bought his taxi years earlier and had made hundreds of trips between Jenin and Ramallah.

Before long, no one was thinking about holiday food or friends. We were all focused on the rain. Less than an hour into the trip, it began pouring. Saleem had to choose between off-road driving, with the risk of getting stuck in the mud, and sticking to the main road, with the chance of getting caught at a checkpoint. Many stationary checkpoints existed at that time, and pop-up checkpoints could appear anywhere.

Neither option was appealing, but Saleem had to decide. "It's raining too hard. We won't be able to make it off road," he stated finally.

I wish the rain had held off for a few more hours, I thought.

In five years in Palestine, I never knew a Palestinian to voice displeasure with rain. Instead, they said, "We love rain. We need it for our trees and our crops."

We proceeded onto a new route that I had not seen before. It was already 2:45 when we reached Jibara checkpoint, south of the city of Tulkarem. The line of cars at the checkpoint was not that long, so we had hope. But many Palestinians were on foot at the crossing, and no one seemed to be moving ahead. The Israeli soldiers were trying to get the people to back up and form a line. They announced several times, "We will start letting you through after you stop the chaos and make a line."

We had waited half an hour or so when Saleem suggested, "Why don't you take our ID cards over to the soldiers and see if you can talk us through?" He had already tried that himself and had been ordered to wait in the van.

I offered, "I can, but usually when I try that, it's useless."

"Just try," he encouraged.

I walked to the soldiers' station and when acknowledged, said, "I am in a taxi with six university students. We are all going to Ramallah. Could we go through now?" I handed him the eight IDs, including Saleem's and mine.

"You can pass, but the others cannot," was the soldier's quick reply.

"But they only want to go home to visit their families. You know there is a holiday beginning tomorrow," I persisted.

"I'm sorry, but they cannot go through. We have our orders not to allow anyone through except people from the neighboring town."

"What if I call the DCO?" I asked, knowing I had contacts at the Israeli District Coordination Office that I had visited each semester while at AAUP.

"You can call the DCO, but they will tell you the same thing. You know the Palestinians go to our settlements and kill people. It is not safe for us, and today, no one is going to pass."

"But they're just students," I pleaded as I found my phone and began dialing the DCO. I spoke to Officer Shiloh, whom I knew, but he only confirmed what I had already been told, that I, but not the students, could pass.

I walked back to the taxi and apologized to everyone as I handed our ID cards back to Saleem. "No way," I reported. "They say no one from Jenin can go through." With the sun already moving to the west, Saleem looked at his watch—3:45—and decided to turn around and try another route.

Around 4:00 p.m. we drove right into another pop-up checkpoint. Saleem braked, and before he had a chance to turn around, the sliding door of our van was jerked open by an Israeli soldier in full camouflage garb, his face painted black, green, and red. He grunted, indicating with his rifle that we should get out. The students stepped down from the van, wondering if this was a joke. Next, my door was opened in the same abrupt manner. Without words, the soldier ordered me outside.

Saleem handed the passports to one of the soldiers, and then he and I joined the students standing on the side of the road. Two of the three soldiers were down on one knee, moving their heads from right to left like troops on enemy territory. Saleem kept repeating the word *tadrib*, meaning drill. Good. It's only a drill, I thought.

"Cynthia!" the third soldier barked at me. I walked over to where he was standing behind the vehicle, out of sight of the others. It was the usual round of questions: "Where are you from? What are you doing here? Where are you going? Who are the people with you? Where are they going?"

I answered all the questions.

"You can pass, but the students cannot," the soldier snapped.

"But we need to go together," I said. "They're just going to visit their families. You know there is a holiday starting tomorrow." But nothing I said made a difference.

Saleem tried to get involved, giving his reasons why they should let us pass, but the soldier growled at him several times, even threatening him if he did not shut his mouth.

We piled into the van and headed back in the direction we had come. It was 4:15, and we had no other roads to try. We were forced to go off road and into the muddy terrain. We sloshed around in the syrupy mud, up inclines and down again, sliding from one side to the other like on an amusement park ride. Saleem skillfully maneuvered the steering wheel and tried to maintain control, but it felt like there was none. We realized we were not going to make it.

When a tractor appeared, ready to pull us along with its thick steel cables, Saleem did not hesitate to accept. The entrepreneurial tractor drivers were in full force that day. As soon as they detached their sturdy cables from one vehicle in trouble, they attached them to another. The field was full of off-road cars. The tractor drivers only got paid a few dollars for their services, but they had a lot of customers. I would pay any amount of money, I thought, to get us all safely home.

Yet even being pulled by the tractor did not provide the assurance I was looking for. I was afraid we were going to tip over as we were pulled up and down several hills. After a mile of that, the tractor driver stopped and quickly unhooked the umbilical cord. I thought it was too soon for him to release us. We still had a major ditch to get through before reaching the edge of the highway.

Despite Saleem's driving expertise, we got stuck. Our wheels spun into the mushy ground, the van going nowhere but down. It was already dark at 5:00 p.m. I had visions of being trapped out there for hours. I was praying, and perhaps Saleem was too, amidst his expletives. Miraculously, the male students, with their good shoes in the mud, put rocks and stones under the wheels, and Saleem drove us out.

We made it onto the road and within ten minutes found ourselves at yet another checkpoint. This one turned out to be more user-friendly. Within twenty minutes, we were allowed through the checkpoint and were on our way home.

At 7:00 in the evening, I walked into the living room of our Ramallah apartment, six hours after leaving Jenin. It had taken six hours to make what should be a two-hour trip. "Are you OK?" Bob asked.

That six-hour trip just a week before Bob and I left Palestine was a reminder of the reality of life for my Palestinian students, colleagues, and friends. The experience said to me, "Remember us. Don't forget what we are going through here, after you are gone."

In thinking back to all my experiences and reflecting on all I learned, nothing stands out more than the resilience of the Palestinian people. This resilience claims, "We will continue living our lives no matter how difficult things may be, no matter what obstacles we face."

Taxi drivers particularly amaze me. They go out of their way to help people get where they need to go, despite the inconvenience or risk to their vehicle. They would never leave a passenger stranded. They are like movie stunt men doing death-defying scenes, except this is real life.

I asked Saleem after we had passed through the final checkpoint, "How does today compare to other travel days for you? Does this kind of thing happen ten percent of the time, twenty percent of the time, or how often?"

Saleem replied, "Today is one of the worst, in the top ten percent. He then proceeded to tell me about his worst day ever, when he spent twelve hours going seventy-five miles from Ramallah to Jenin, only to end up back home, never having arrived. "That was the worst," he said and smiled.

Israeli soldiers in army jeeps and trucks at pop-up checkpoints

Israeli soldiers in tanks moving dirt around to restrict movement

The separation wall (Cynthia standing by wall, top right)

Olive picking—Bob (top), Cynthia and Amal (bottom)

ELC rooftop party—Wafa (top) and Leen (bottom)

Wildflowers in Palestine

AAUP community honoring Waleed Deeb's five years of service

2004 graduates Mahmoud and Subhi with Michelle and Cynthia

Cynthia's students (2004 graduates)—twins Qusai and Qais

Cynthia and Bob in a Palestinian home

Epilogue

In the fall of 2020, the Arab American University of Palestine celebrated its twentieth year. Over the past twenty years, the university has been thriving and growing. Five men have served as president. Student enrollment has grown from about 350 the first year to more than 10,000 today. Faculty members have increased from fewer than 30 to more than 450. A new branch campus in Ramallah houses graduate programs. On the Jenin campus, the original four buildings have blossomed into dozens. My Palestinian friends who still work there tell me that I would not recognize the campus.

In twenty years, more than 18,000 students have graduated from the university, more than 50% female. The AAUP website (aaup.edu) features a photo gallery and tens of success stories from graduates, including students that I taught. Alumni are working successfully in their careers in varied fields, both in Palestine and abroad. Many have completed graduate degrees. Staying in touch with a number of students, as well as faculty and staff, is an ongoing reward for me.

When I communicate with a Palestinian friend, I usually ask about the political situation. There have been many ups and downs since I left Palestine. Even when things seem better, meaning fewer checkpoints, for one thing, the reality is that Palestinians continue to live under military occupation. As one friend recently put it, "We are oppressed every second." Yet they carry on. I continue to hope for their freedom.

Aerial view of AAUP in 2020

Arab American University in 2020

Acknowledgments

Many people helped me with this memoir. I am grateful to each one, including those who remain unnamed to protect their identities.

I am grateful to the teachers and staff I worked with in Palestine who helped me reflect, express memories, and check facts: Lamees Abbas, Mervat Aiash, Leen Al-Masri, Kawther Al-Shareef, Suzanne Belleci, Susan Bertoni, Waleed Deeb, Robert Gravelin, Leanne Hagglund, Samah Khalaf, Sarah Martin, Michelle Plunkett, Lasse Schmidt, Barbara Settles, Jonathan Smith, and James Thomas.

I am thankful to my very first readers in 2006: my aunt, Evie Yoder Miller, and Mary Ann Zehr, my longtime friend who read multiple drafts. The affirmation of both women gave me the courage to move ahead.

I thank dear friends who read drafts in part or in whole and offered their insights and suggestions: Suzanne Belleci, Waleed Deeb, Peg Engle, Doreen Ewert, Kathy Fisher, Judy Gingerich, Robert Gravelin, Nahed Habiballah, Patti Helton, Lisa Schirch, Barbara Settles, Jonathan Smith, Mary Sprunger, James Thomas, Lisa Wilder, and Linda Work.

Special thanks to the people from those named above who read more than one draft and/or advised me in the final stages. The time I spent with each of them online over several months during the Covid-19 pandemic was one of the great pleasures of working on this book.

Thank you to those who provided space for the writing process: the guys at Auski Camp in Dahab, Egypt; Elisabeth Yoder and Wahba Ayyad in Cairo, Egypt; my brother and sister-in-law Terry and Joan Gotwals Yoder in Leola, Pennsylvania; Samuel and Georgie Martin in Lancaster, Pennsylvania; my parents Ed and Theo Yoder in Archbold, Ohio and Fremont, Indiana; my brother-in-law and sister-in-law Denis and Kate Gravelin in Colchester, Vermont; and my father-in-law and mother-in-law Albert and Yvonne Gravelin in Burlington, Vermont.

I got inspiration during the pandemic from weekly swims at Xote Aquatic park and hikes at El Charco del Ingenio botanical garden, both in San Miguel de Allende, Mexico.

Thanks to my friend, Andrea Wallpe, who shared what she knew about the publishing process.

I am indebted to my friend, Mark Sunderman, who spent hours searching through boxes and files in my Athens, Ohio storage unit when I was in Mexico and unable to travel to Ohio due to the coronavirus. He retrieved and sent me needed documents that I did not have in cyber space.

Thank you to the folks at EbookPbook who assisted with interior text formatting, ebook conversion, and the cover. Thank you to Gerardo Espinosa, who helped with our homemade map.

I am grateful to my colleagues at the Arab American University, those who welcomed me as an international faculty member and those who worked with me in the English Language Center. Thank you to Najat Rahman, who hired both my husband and me. If not for her, Bob and I would not have met. Above all, thanks to Waleed Deeb, for his trust in me and the support and friendship he has provided over the years.

I am equally grateful to my students at AAUP who taught me to listen, to laugh, and to better understand the situation in Palestine.

I am thankful for each Palestinian person who welcomed me into his or her home and heart. Only a few are mentioned by name in this book, but there were many more. I will not forget their amazing warmth and hospitality.

I thank my family and my friends who provided so much support while I lived in Palestine. Their emails, letters, and calls meant the world to me. The hand-written letters written by my nieces and nephews in their children's voices are a special treasure.

Most of all, I thank my spouse and biggest fan, Bob Gravelin, who encouraged me to write this book. He not only cheered me on as a writer but also read several drafts himself, listened while I read out loud, and gave invaluable feedback. In the final stages, he helped with maps, photos, cover design, layout, formatting, and publishing. Throughout, he provided food, drink, quirky comments about the wayfaring writer's workshop, laughter, breaks, music, and massages, even after 9:00 p.m.

Notes

1. "Palestinian Refugees." *Anti-Defamation League.* www.adl.org/resources/glossary-terms/palestinian-refugees. Accessed 30 September 2020.
2. "Special Statistical Bulletin on the 65th Anniversary of the Palestinian Nakba." *Palestinian Central Bureau of Statistics.* www.pcbs.gov.ps/portals/_pcbs/PressRelease/Press_En_nakba65E.pdf. Accessed 30 September 2020.
3. "The Question of Palestine." *The United Nations.* www.un.org/unispal/history. Accessed 30 September 2020.
4. "Intifada Toll 2000 – 2005." *BBC News, 8 February 2005.* news.bbc.co.uk/2/hi/middle_east/3694350.stm. Accessed 9 November 2020.
5. "Who We Are: Palestine Refugees." *United Nations Relief and Works Agency for Palestine Refugees in the Near East.* www.unrwa.org/who-we-are. Accessed 30 September 2020.
6. "Who We Are: Palestine Refugees." *United Nations Relief and Works Agency for Palestine Refugees in the Near East.* www.unrwa.org/who-we-are. Accessed 30 September 2020.
7. "Jenin Camp." *United Nations Relief and Works Agency for Palestine Refugees in the Near East.* www.unrwa.org/where-we-work/west-bank/jenin-camp. Accessed 30 September 2020.

8. Bennet, James. "Death on the Campus: Jenin; UN Report Rejects Claims of a Massacre." 2 August 2002. *The New York Times.* www.nytimes.com/2002/08/02/world/death-on-the-campus-jenin-un-report-rejects-claims-of-a-massacre-of-refugees.html. Accessed 30 September 2020.
9. "Jenin Camp." *United Nations Relief and Works Agency for Palestine Refugees in the Near East.* www.unrwa.org/where-we-work/west-bank/jenin-camp. Accessed 30 September 2020.
10. "Israel Demographics." *World Population Review.* worldpopulationreview.com/countries/israel-population. Accessed 30 September 2020.
11. "Israel Demographics." *World Population Review.* worldpopulationreview.com/countries/israel-population. Accessed 30 September 2020.
12. "The World Factbook: Middle East: West Bank: People and Society." *Central Intelligence Agency.* www.cia.gov/library/publications/the-world-factbook/geos/we.html. Accessed 30 September 2020.

A Glossary of Arabic Terms

RELIGIOUS TERMS AND EXPRESSIONS

Allah – God
Allah ma'akum – May God be with you.
Allah yarhamu – May God have mercy on his soul.
Allah yarhamha – May God have mercy on her soul.
Al-Aqsa – Islamic holy site in Jerusalem
Al-baqi fi hayatik – May the rest of his or her life be lived in yours.
Alhamdullilah – Thank God. Thanks be to God.
Al-Haram Al-Sharif — Islamic holy site in Jerusalem
Azama Allah ajrukum – May God reward you.
Bismallah al-rahman al-raheem – In the name of God, the most gracious, the most merciful
Eid Al-Adha – Islamic Feast of the Sacrifice
hajj – Islamic pilgrimage to Mecca
haram – forbidden by Allah, against the laws of God
hijab – Islamic head covering for women
iftar – Islamic fast-breaking meal
Insha Allah – God willing
jilbab – Islamic long, loose garment for women
Kul min Allah – Everything is from God.
Masha Allah – expression of joy, praise, or thankfulness
muhajaba – a woman wearing the *hijab*

OTHER TERMS AND EXPRESSIONS

ajaaneb – foreigners
Al-Muntada – The Young Scientists Club
Al-Nakba – The Catastrophe, 1948 displacement of Palestinians
Al-Wade' – The Situation
Habibi – a term of endearment said to a man
Habibti – a term of endearment said to a woman
Haik al-haya – This is life.
intifada – shaking off, uprising
Itfaddalu – Welcome. Please. (an offer of food, drink, etc.)
jaysh – army, soldiers
keffiyeh – checkered scarf worn around the head or neck
Mabruk – Congratulations!
Marhaba – Hello.
Mish maoul – unbelievable, I cannot believe it!
Sabah al-khayr – Good morning.
servees – a shared taxi
shekel – currency of Israel and the Palestinian Territory
shekleen – two shekels
Shu hanamil – What can we do? What shall we do?
Shukran — Thank you.
tadrib – training, a drill
Yalla – Let's go! Come on!

GREETINGS AND RESPONSES

A: *Salam alaykum* – Peace be upon you.
B: *Wa alaykum as-salam* – And on you, peace.
A: *Hamdillah as-salameh* – Thank God for your safety.
B: *Allah ye salmik* – May God give you peace.

FOODS

baba ghanouj – mashed cooked eggplant with tahini
falafel – fried ground chickpea balls
hummus – mashed cooked chickpeas with tahini
khubezeh – mallow
kufta – meatballs
maftul – dish of rolled wheat served with broth
marameyya – the herb sage
mujadara – rice and lentil dish
musakhan – sumac chicken and flatbread dish
tahini – sesame seed paste
shish taouk – chicken kebab
wara aineb – stuffed grape leaves
zeit wa zaatar – olive oil and thyme

About the Author

Cynthia D. Yoder grew up in Archbold, Ohio. She received a B.A. from Goshen College and an M.A. from Indiana University. Her career as an English language teacher has involved classroom teaching, professional development for teachers, curriculum development, and program administration in seven countries: Egypt, Palestine, Romania, Kuwait, Sri Lanka, Japan, and the United States. In the U.S., she has taught at Indiana University, Ohio University, and Eastern Mennonite University. Her avocations include creating photo books of her experiences in each country and writing informal family history books. She lives in San Miguel de Allende, Mexico with her husband, Robert Gravelin, a painter and musician.

www.ingramcontent.com/pod-product-compliance
Lightning Source LLC
Chambersburg PA
CBHW020904080526
44589CB00011B/443